## Dorset
Edited by Jessica Woodbridge

First published in Great Britain in 2005 by:
Young Writers
Remus House
Coltsfoot Drive
Peterborough
PE2 9JX
Telephone: 01733 890066
Website: www.youngwriters.co.uk

All Rights Reserved

© Copyright Contributors 2005

SB ISBN 1 84602 144 8

# Foreword

Young Writers was established in 1991 and has been passionately devoted to the promotion of reading and writing in children and young adults ever since. The quest continues today. Young Writers remains as committed to the fostering of burgeoning poetic and literary talent as ever.

This year's Young Writers competition has proven as vibrant and dynamic as ever and we are delighted to present a showcase of the best poetry from across the UK. Each poem has been carefully selected from a wealth of *Playground Poets* entries before ultimately being published in this, our thirteenth primary school poetry series.

Once again, we have been supremely impressed by the overall high quality of the entries we have received. The imagination, energy and creativity which has gone into each young writer's entry made choosing the best poems a challenging and often difficult but ultimately hugely rewarding task - the general high standard of the work submitted amply vindicating this opportunity to bring their poetry to a larger appreciative audience.

We sincerely hope you are pleased with our final selection and that you will enjoy *Playground Poets Dorset* for many years to come.

# Contents

**All Saints CE VC Primary School**

| | |
|---|---|
| Bethany Scott (11) | 1 |
| Luke Rendall (11) | 1 |
| Bethany Spicer (10) | 2 |
| Betony Clasby (11) | 2 |
| Harry Brown (10) | 2 |
| Steven Saywell (11) | 3 |
| Joe Yandell (9) | 3 |
| Craig Tite (11) | 3 |
| Rebekah White (10) | 4 |
| Edward Trist (10) | 4 |
| Lucy Jones (10) | 5 |
| Sammy Paull (11) | 5 |
| Richard Jenkins (9) | 5 |
| Kelly Foot (11) | 6 |
| Holly Tamlyn (11) | 6 |
| Mycroft Watts (11) | 7 |
| Ben Murcer (10) | 7 |
| Jade Bailey (9) | 7 |

**Canford Heath Middle School**

| | |
|---|---|
| Stephanie Ross (8) | 8 |
| Thomas Loe (10) | 9 |
| Arianne Oliver (9) | 10 |
| Nathan Jones (10) | 10 |
| Jed Briant (10) | 11 |
| Shannon Perry (8) | 11 |
| Lewis Lindsay (10) | 12 |
| Damaris Trujillo (9) | 12 |
| Anna Watton (10) | 13 |
| Lewis Blackmore (10) | 13 |
| Chloe Marie Halfhide (10) | 14 |
| Emily Hodges (9) | 15 |
| Emma Turner (10) | 16 |
| Nikita Best (9) | 16 |
| Hannah Hickman (9) | 17 |
| Megan Philpott (10) | 17 |
| Laura Cox (9) | 18 |

**Christchurch Junior School**
  Zoë Seabourne  (8) — 18
  Bethan Collingwood  (11) — 19
  Lucy Du Cros  (9) — 19
  Nicole Feeley  (10) — 20
  Holly Du Cros  (9) — 20
  Kate Wyles  (10) — 21
  Eva Cheeseman  (10) — 21
  Leanne Faulkner  (11) — 22
  Lyam Galpin  (11) — 22
  Charlotte Lowe  (11) — 23
  Kelly Way  (10) — 23
  Bailey Melvin-Teng  (10) — 24
  Jennifer Gee  (11) — 25
  Lauren Burnley  (10) — 26
  Ellie Lovett  (11) — 27

**Christ the King RC Primary School**
  Samuel Bush  (8) — 27
  Dale Adamson  (10) — 28
  Daisy Lapworth  (7) — 28
  Jordan Bell  (11) — 29
  Megan Rose Davis  (7) — 29
  Megan Barrington  (10) — 30
  Shelby Fiorentini  (8) — 30
  Mercedes Apps  (10) — 31
  Alisha Aragones  (8) — 31
  Callum Cooper  (8) — 32
  Christina Murphy  (8) — 32
  Joshua Manzi  (11) — 33
  Anthony Grieve  (10) — 33
  Ryan Hoff  (11) — 34
  Joanna Treggiden  (10) — 35
  Oliver Moyse  (10) — 36
  Shelby Richardson  (11) — 36
  Kelly-Marie Dady  (11) — 37
  Liam Giffin  (11) — 37
  Rebecca Watts  (10) — 38
  Jack Whitton  (10) — 38
  Alexander Reeves  (10) — 39
  David Cherrett  (10) — 39

| | |
|---|---|
| Gabrielle Excell  (10) | 40 |
| Sarah Comerford  (9) | 40 |
| Sophie Robinson  (9) | 41 |
| Sophie Batty  (10) | 41 |
| Nicole Allen  (9) | 42 |
| Carlos Aragones  (10) | 42 |
| Micky Edwards  (10) | 43 |
| Robert Herbert  (9) | 43 |
| Marco Bolt  (10) | 44 |
| Francesca Young  (9) | 44 |
| Lucy Field  (10) | 44 |
| Jenna Cornick  (8) | 45 |
| Melissa Biddlecombe  (9) | 45 |
| Poppy Brock  (9) | 46 |
| David Long  (9) | 46 |

**Hillbourne Middle School**

| | |
|---|---|
| Andrew Manston  (9) | 46 |
| Thomas Lovell  (8) | 47 |
| Ryan Copleston  (11) | 47 |
| Holly Grant & Adam Wood  (9) | 48 |
| Kiarna Ducker  (11) | 48 |
| Jordan Witt  (9) | 49 |
| Jade Davis  (8) | 49 |
| Daniel Winwood  (10) | 50 |
| Hannah Whatley  (9) | 50 |
| Rachel Lye  (10) | 51 |
| Scarlett Adams  (9) | 51 |
| Katie Bligh  (10) | 52 |
| Thomas Holden  (10) | 52 |
| Lydia Proudley & Melissa Buckland  (9) | 52 |
| Connor Dyke  (9) | 53 |
| Olivia Coles  (9) | 53 |
| Joseph Benham  (10) | 53 |
| Aimee Auger  (9) | 54 |
| Jordan Bromley  (10) | 54 |
| Thomas Legg  (10) | 55 |
| Jade Fudge  (11) | 55 |
| Abbie McKenna  (9) | 56 |
| Ashleigh Phillips  (9) | 56 |
| Eleanor Pickford  (9) | 57 |

| | |
|---|---|
| Natasha Carter  (9) | 57 |
| Fleur Yeats  (10) | 58 |
| Jessica Longstaff  (11) | 58 |
| Michael Sneddon  (11) | 59 |
| Lauren Belben  (9) | 59 |
| Tanvir Ahmed & Chris Gloster  (9) | 60 |
| Sarah Benfield  (10) | 60 |
| Tia Druce  (8) & Charlie Triggs  (9) | 60 |
| Jessica Nash  (8) & Philippe Lord  (9) | 61 |
| Rebekah Kerr  (8) & Maxine Wilson  (9) | 61 |
| Sophie Allisett  (10) | 62 |

**Port Regis School**

| | |
|---|---|
| Danielle Wickham  (9) | 62 |
| Sophie Geikie-Cobb  (7) | 63 |
| Halimah Schmidt  (10) | 63 |
| Anastasia Mackaness  (9) | 64 |
| Freddie Ball  (10) | 64 |
| Hannah Bonnell  (11) | 65 |
| Nicholas Evans  (10) | 65 |
| Emily Watts  (10) | 66 |
| Harry Waddington  (10) | 66 |
| Ella Spottiswood  (11) | 67 |
| Lloyd Wallace  (9) | 67 |
| Christopher Brinkworth  (11) | 68 |
| Jack Robinson  (10) | 68 |
| Freddie Ashford-Russell  (10) | 68 |
| Matilda Wilkinson  (10) | 69 |
| Connie Robins  (9) | 69 |
| Lucy Allison  (10) | 70 |
| William von Behr  (11) | 70 |
| Flora McFarlane  (10) | 71 |
| Ben Willbourn  (9) | 71 |
| Emily Matthews  (10) | 72 |
| Hanifah Debono  (11) | 72 |
| Scarlett Aichroth  (9) | 73 |
| Henry Turpie  (10) | 73 |
| Thomas Mitchell  (10) | 74 |
| Harriet Hedges  (11) | 74 |
| Jamie Horton  (9) | 75 |
| Kathryn Francis  (10) | 75 |

Elizabeth Killick  (9) — 76
Anders Horwood  (9) — 76
Patrick Milne  (10) — 77
Tim Dickins  (10) — 77
Edward MacDonald  (9) — 78
Robin Brinkworth  (9) — 78
Jack Gething  (9) — 79
Natasha O'Keeffe  (9) — 79
William Roberts  (9) — 80
Oscar Appleby  (10) — 80
Paul Collins  (9) — 81
Anna Gray  (9) — 81
Milly Hedges  (9) — 82
Morgan Cronin-Webb  (10) — 82
Holly Isard  (11) — 83
Eleanor Thwaites  (9) — 84

**St Michael's Primary School, Lyme Regis**
Connor Pemberton  (10) — 84
Bethany Allen  (10) — 85
Henry Wadsworth  (9) — 85
Jessie Parker  (10) — 86
Liam Trice  (9) — 86
Sarah Nicholson  (9) — 86
Brady Wright  (9) — 87
Zachary Rees-Haughton  (9) — 87
Jack Chan  (9) — 87
Lorrayne White  (10) — 88
Oscar Gordon-Christopher  (10) — 88
Rachael Tipping  (10) — 89
Archie Stoke Faiers  (9) — 90
Dominic Kirtley  (10) — 90

**St Thomas Garnet's School, Bournemouth**
Philipp Antonas  (10) — 90
Edward Parker  (10) — 91
Bryony Cook  (11) — 91
Amber Porter  (8) — 92
William Porter  (11) — 92
Daniel Doherty  (10) — 93
Robert Degan  (11) — 93

| | |
|---|---|
| Hannah Doyle  (9) | 94 |
| Rebecca Lucy Murphy  (10) | 94 |
| Matthew Giddens  (7) | 95 |
| Lewis Hawkins  (8) | 95 |
| Amber Cook  (9) | 96 |
| Allie Kenward  (10) | 96 |
| Jasmine Elliot  (10) | 97 |
| Katie Spencer  (9) | 97 |
| Jessica Smith  (10) | 97 |
| Harriett Wragg  (9) | 98 |
| Kate Glanville  (7) | 98 |
| Jean-Jacques Coppini  (8) | 99 |
| Jack Palmer  (10) | 99 |
| Landi Wagner  (10) | 100 |
| Jessica Balfour  (7) | 101 |
| Taylor Rees  (8) | 101 |
| Diarmid Becker  (8) | 101 |
| Nadia Foy  (8) | 102 |
| Christie Quinn  (8) | 103 |
| Amy Mack Nava  (8) | 104 |
| Charles Tizzard  (8) | 104 |
| Henry Newton  (9) | 104 |
| Alexander Drake  (8) | 105 |
| Catherine Shelton  (9) | 106 |
| Maria Degan  (9) | 106 |
| Alexandra Hibberd  (8) | 107 |
| Ersan Beskardes  (9) | 107 |
| Oliver Yeadon  (8) | 108 |

**Salway Ash CE VA Primary School**

| | |
|---|---|
| Joshua Green  (11) | 108 |
| Matthew Pyett  (10) | 109 |
| Blaine Davis  (10) | 109 |
| Jack Hill  (10) | 110 |
| George Sparks  (10) | 110 |
| Laura Alexander  (10) | 111 |
| Aidan Simson  (10) | 111 |
| Jessica Kennedy  (10) | 112 |
| Katrina Roberts  (10) | 112 |
| Holly Parkes  (10) | 113 |
| Marcus Crew  (10) | 113 |

| | |
|---|---|
| Ben Hawkins  (11) | 114 |
| Callum Flawn  (9) | 114 |
| Jordon Taylor  (9) | 114 |
| Abigail Hoskins  (9) | 115 |
| Spike Duff  (9) | 115 |
| Jamal Hadj-Aissa  (10) | 115 |
| Amy Bodycombe  (10) | 116 |
| Alicia Chambers-Hill  (10) | 116 |
| Mini Warren  (11) | 116 |
| Joshua Baker  (10) | 117 |
| Joshua Sprague  (10) | 117 |
| Adam Rhodes  (9) | 117 |
| Naomi Davidson  (10) | 118 |
| Gemma Smith  (11) | 118 |

**Sandford St Martin's CE VA First School**

| | |
|---|---|
| Carla Jordan  (8) | 119 |
| Connie Woodworth  (8) | 119 |
| Jacob Rolls  (7) | 120 |
| Jennifer Auger  (7) | 120 |
| Amy Shepherd  (8) | 121 |
| Remy White  (7) | 121 |
| Charlie Jones  (7) | 122 |
| Thomas Hawkins  (8) | 122 |
| Ryan Adams  (7) | 122 |
| Dylan Crook  (7) | 123 |
| Elli Masterton  (7) | 123 |
| Harry Rose  (7) | 123 |
| Amber Jackson  (8) | 124 |
| Amber Baker  (7) | 124 |
| Bethan Harcourt  (8) | 125 |
| Oliver Meaden  (7) | 125 |
| James Blakesley  (8) | 126 |
| Sarah Richards  (7) | 126 |
| Emily-Jayne Court  (8) | 127 |
| Amy Hallett  (8) | 127 |
| Tom Henstridge  (8) | 128 |
| Sidney Burgess  (7) | 128 |
| Danielle Wills  (8) | 129 |
| Ashleigh Jo Hall  (8) | 129 |
| Jade Fowler  (8) | 130 |

| | |
|---|---:|
| Stephanie Lamb (8) | 130 |
| Amy Webb (8) | 131 |
| Henry Keep (7) | 131 |
| Casey Medley (7) | 132 |
| Ben Williams (7) | 132 |
| Will Joyce (7) | 133 |
| Nathan Lee-Blues (8) | 133 |
| Stephanie Howard (7) | 134 |
| Emily Kennedy (8) | 134 |
| Jade-Marie Shilling (7) | 135 |
| Jamie Harkins (7) | 135 |
| Rhiannon Davies (8) | 136 |
| Daniel Bray (8) | 136 |

**The Priory CE VA Primary School**

| | |
|---|---:|
| Alanna Sibbald (10) | 137 |
| Abbie Denison (9) | 137 |
| Jack Brickell (9) | 138 |
| George Burgess (9) | 138 |
| Abigail Watts (9) | 139 |
| Olivia Bisson-Simmonds (10) | 140 |
| Sophie Pope (10) | 141 |
| Lauren Beech (9) | 142 |
| Isobel Booth (8) | 142 |
| Joanna Wassell (10) | 143 |
| Elizabeth Lovett (8) | 143 |
| Jim Gerrard (10) | 144 |
| Jake Fell (10) | 144 |
| Rebecca Simpson (10) | 145 |
| Elliot Wilks (9) | 145 |
| Emily Fardell (10) | 146 |
| Emily Gola (9) | 146 |
| Sam Pitman (10) | 147 |
| Louis Rice (10) | 147 |
| Nicola Brown (10) | 148 |
| Lucy Cherrett (8) | 148 |
| Lydia Bassett (9) | 149 |
| Aaron Rackstraw (10) | 149 |
| Cloe Brunerie (10) | 150 |
| Hannah Arkell (10) | 151 |
| Joseph Alexander (10) | 151 |

| | |
|---|---|
| Jordan Puttick  (9) | 152 |
| Melissa Stocker  (8) | 152 |
| India Dale  (10) | 153 |
| Edward Burt  (8) | 153 |
| Callum Heath  (10) | 154 |
| Rachel Hawkins  (8) | 154 |
| Mason Doick  (10) | 155 |

# The Poems

## The Copycat

My neighbour is a copycat,
She does everything I do,
When I do the gardening,
She does it too.

When I went round her house,
She fell down the stairs,
She went to hospital,
She was quite scared,
She had never done anything on her own,
Until I said, 'You've broke a bone.'

So now she never copies,
She does her own thing,
When I do the washing,
She does the shopping.

When I go out,
She walks about,
When I eat,
She cuts the meat.

I go to bed,
She hugs her ted,
I go to sleep,
She does a leap.

**Bethany Scott (11)**
All Saints CE VC Primary School

## The Penguin On The Go

There once was a penguin from Iceland,
Who visited his friend from Thailand,
When he finally got back,
His mum gave him a big smack,
So he flew to his dad in Ireland.

**Luke Rendall (11)**
All Saints CE VC Primary School

## A Man Called Paul

There once was a man called Paul,
Who unfortunately grew very tall,
So he sat in the sink,
Cos he wanted to shrink,
But he grew to the size of a wall.

**Bethany Spicer (10)**
**All Saints CE VC Primary School**

## Down In The Ocean Blue

Down in the ocean blue,
Where no one has ever ventured,
A turtle swims, cruising the waves,
Going into underwater caves.
Further down in that ocean blue,
A gentle whale gracefully glides,
And makes a surprise,
On some small green plankton,
Drifting high in that ocean blue.

**Betony Clasby (11)**
**All Saints CE VC Primary School**

## Debbie The Sheep

Debbie's wool is like brushed hair,
Her bleat is a foghorn,
Her hooves grip like tyres,
And her eyes are as shiny as stars.

**Harry Brown (10)**
**All Saints CE VC Primary School**

## Summer

Summer's here,
Summer's there,
Summer's everywhere.
Spring has gone,
Autumn is not long,
And winter is far gone.

**Steven Saywell (11)**
**All Saints CE VC Primary School**

## Sports

Football's fun
Netball's nice
Rugby's rough
Hockey's hot
Swimming's sweet
Cricket's cool
Fishing's fine
Riding rocks
Golf's good.

**Joe Yandell (9)**
**All Saints CE VC Primary School**

## Christmas - Cinquain

Turkey,
Loads of presents,
Sherry and hot mince pies,
Santa Claus coming in the night,
*Christmas!*

**Craig Tite (11)**
**All Saints CE VC Primary School**

## Horse ABC

A is for Appaloosa, as sweet as candy
B is for Belgian Draft horse, big and fluffy
C is for Clydesdale, ginger and smart
D is for Dartmoor, pulling a cart
E is for energy nuts, yummy and crunchy
F is for Fallabela, running around the country
G is for geldings, pacing the fence,
H is for hunting, it makes a lot of sense
I is for improving the horses' behaviour
J is for jeep, looking like a caver
K is for kicking, horses always do that
L is for lead rope on the mat
M is for Mustang, wild and free
N is for New Forest, chasing a buzzy bee
O is for oats, ponies love them
P is for Piebald by the River Thames
Q is for quad sounding its horn
R is for Roan that's just been born
S is for Shire, heavy and big
T is for treat, like a fig
U is for unsteady, when they've got a sore foot
V is for vehicle, covered in soot
W is for walk around the sea deck,
X is for X-ray for a broken neck
Y is for yard, what a boring sight
Z is for zebra, stripy, black and white.

**Rebekah White (10)**
**All Saints CE VC Primary School**


## A Parrot's House

There once was a parrot from York,
Who lived in a house made of chalk,
But whenever it rained,
Then he always complained,
So he filled up the holes with caulk.

**Edward Trist (10)**
**All Saints CE VC Primary School**

## Summertime

Summertime
Flowers out
No ice now
Just sunshine
Play football
In the park
Green ice cream
Yum, yum, yum!

**Lucy Jones (10)**
All Saints CE VC Primary School

## Horses

H ay in the net
O ver the jumps
R iding through snow
S hoes clattering
E ating the grass
S tables are waiting.

**Sammy Paull (11)**
All Saints CE VC Primary School

## Lessons

History is hopeful,
Geography is good,
Maths is magic,
Crafts if I could,
ICT is cool,
RE is raging,
Drama is an act,
Literacy is paging.

**Richard Jenkins (9)**
All Saints CE VC Primary School

## I Thought I Saw . . .

I thought I saw,
What I think I see,
A furry little bumblebee,
Flying by me.

I think I see,
What I thought I saw,
A little wolf,
At my door.

I scream and I shout,
And I run about,
The wolf chases me round,
So soon I feel dizzy and fall to the ground.

**Kelly Foot (11)**
**All Saints CE VC Primary School**


## Normal Day

Get out of the car,
Go inside,
Mum has her,
Cup of tea,
Go upstairs,
Race the dog,
Now get changed,
Go downstairs,
Dog has barked,
Excited,
It's time for,
 . . . *Walkies.*

**Holly Tamlyn (11)**
**All Saints CE VC Primary School**

## Lessons

History, music, ICT,
Drama, English and DT,
It has a sudden change, you see,
From fun and games to Key Stage 3,
All the lessons aren't easy, *boo hoo!*
But they're fun to learn.
*A big whoo hoo!*

**Mycroft Watts (11)**
**All Saints CE VC Primary School**

## Football Skills

Football rocks,
Steve does not,
My best friend
Scores in one shot,
He is so hot,
But I am not.

**Ben Murcer (10)**
**All Saints CE VC Primary School**

## The Man On The Moon

There once was a man on the moon,
Who got married to a baboon,
The wedding was not good,
We never understood,
The sad divorce came very soon.

**Jade Bailey (9)**
**All Saints CE VC Primary School**

## Boring Babysitters

My old babysitter Emma,
It was a horrible dilemma,
She doesn't like my pet,
She'd better regret,
My old babysitter Emma.

My recent babysitter Chloe,
She hit my sister Zoe,
My mum got cross,
To show who's boss,
My recent babysitter Chloe.

My dreadful babysitter Sarah,
I just couldn't bare her,
She was disgustingly mean,
Spotty not clean,
My dreadful babysitter Sarah.

My gruesome babysitter Claire,
Make her angry I dare,
She comes extra late,
Followed by her mate,
My gruesome babysitter Claire.

My ugly babysitter Mandy,
She won't stop chewing candy,
Her teeth are black,
Some are cracked,
My ugly babysitter Mandy.

Last but not least,
My babysitter Clarise,
She's better than the rest,
She's simply the best,
My babysitter Clarise.

**Stephanie Ross (8)**
**Canford Heath Middle School**

## The Rainforest

Deep inside the forest,
Where you see the tiger's eye,
Deep inside the forest,
Where the birds fly high.

The gracefulness of the birds,
The mightiness of the apes,
The trees shadow the ground,
Like a thick, dark cape.

Now inside the forest,
The animals start to run,
Now inside the forest,
The bulldozers have come.

The colours of the treetops,
The bareness of the ground,
Listen to the bushes,
You can hardly hear a sound.

Suddenly, a shadow,
Hiding in a tree,
It's running away from something,
I hope it's not me.

How can they destroy this paradise?
To the animals it's one big house,
From the bold and beautiful tiger,
To the timid and tiniest mouse.

Deep inside the forest,
Where you see the tiger's eye,
Deep inside the forest,
Where the birds fly high.

**Thomas Loe (10)**
**Canford Heath Middle School**

## The Park

To the park I go one day,
I wonder just how long we'll stay,
To swing on swings,
And slide on slides,
I cannot count how many times.

The roundabout goes round and round,
Whilst the football needs to be found,
The children laugh and run around,
Oh they can make such a sound.

Time for a drink and something to eat,
Remembering to sit at the provided seat,
Rubbish in the bin,
Oh what's that din?
The boys are now kicking a tin.

It's getting late,
So we close the gate,
And head off home before it gets too late.

**Arianne Oliver (9)**
**Canford Heath Middle School**


## Tyrannosaurus Rex

His eyes are as big as grey stones,
His jaw is as long as a human rib bone,
His teeth are as long as an ice cream cone,
His head is as hard as a rock all alone.

His arms are as short as a phone,
His body is as big as the Millennium Dome,
His legs are as big as a jungle tree,
His tail is as long as a Brachiosaurus' knee.

His ribs are as long as a giant banana,
His claws are as long as a piranha,
His tongue is as long as a sausage,
His brain is as thick as a blockage.

**Nathan Jones (10)**
**Canford Heath Middle School**

## War!

War is something nobody likes,
War, war, it's a thing you'd hate,
Nobody likes to fight,
You get yourself in a dirty state!

My brother says, 'War is awesome,'
My mum says, 'War is bad,'
My sister says, 'Go away,'
My dad says, 'War is rad.'

I'd hate to go to war,
I really think I'd die,
My dad said he would win,
Knowing him he'd probably cry!

I'd love to watch my dad,
He thinks he'd be so cool,
But he'd probably get hit,
In the head with a big, fat tool!

**Jed Briant (10)**
**Canford Heath Middle School**


## Friendly People!

My mother, she's a very fine lady,
My father is full of hopes and maybes,
My brother, well! he's a pest,
My grandad, well, he's the best,
My nanny is just a very kind lady,
My uncle acts just like a baby,
My family's cool,
And I'm the best,
So come and see us,
Be our guests.

**Shannon Perry (8)**
**Canford Heath Middle School**

## I'm A Poet And I Didn't Even Know It

One goal! Two goals! Three goals! Four!
All I hear is Fergie knocking on the door!
He wants us to see Scholes,
About these goals,
He hasn't been scoring,
So it's getting kind of boring.

When Beckham left us he took the 12.30 bus,
But now we've got Ronaldo to take his place,
So we can continue with the title race.

Man U, Man U is our name,
Man U, Man U is our game,
Man U, Man U are the best,
Man U, Man U, better than the rest.

Rooney, Rooney go for gold,
That move to United wasn't bold,
Rio, Rio what shall he do?
5 year contract, it's all up to you,
75 grand,
Paid in hand,
To recover from this band.

**Lewis Lindsay (10)**
**Canford Heath Middle School**


## Springtime

Spring always hits my eyes,
While I see them in disguise,
The petals reach the sky on a flight,
While I see them blue and white.

Animals come out to play,
Throughout the long and graceful day.

We're going on holiday,
Jamaica I say,
It's so much fun, *hooray, hooray!*

**Damaris Trujillo (9)**
**Canford Heath Middle School**

## Games

When you get hit,
You are on it.

'Tag' is just the same,
It is just a game.

'Stuck in the mud' is fun,
But only if you have one.

Football is cool,
Only if you learn at school.

Let people play,
So they don't get in the way.

You can play basketball,
Only if you are tall.

If your name is Dennis,
You will be very good at tennis.

Dancing is prancing in the air,
But only if you have tied your hair.

**Anna Watton (10)**
**Canford Heath Middle School**


## My Accident

A great day dawns -
Paintballing,
*Hooray!*
In the woods,
Get the gear,
Find a place to hide,
Or you'll get hit,
Stay there,
I'm going,
Ooowwww!
I got shot in the eye,
I'm not doing that again!

**Lewis Blackmore (10)**
**Canford Heath Middle School**

## My Mum Has Gone Crazy

She scares all the birds in the park,
How embarrassing is that?
She's always mucking around when we're shopping,
She even fell asleep on the cat.

Why does my mum have to be crazy?
Why does it always have to be me?
She has a relative but I'm not sure who,
She's so crazy, it could very well be a key.

Her hair is full of knots,
She'd dyed her hair blue and pink,
How embarrassing is that?
She never has any time to think.

She met her friend in the park,
Who was also very crazy,
She was just like my mum,
My mum's friend is really lazy.

Guess how she met her friend; or could it be a relative?
She had an enormous blister,
Just like my mum,
And she turned out to be her sister.

**Chloe Marie Halfhide (10)**
**Canford Heath Middle School**

# Heathland

Come on all you people, walk along the heath,
Come and smell the flowers,
And watch the tall trees,
Sway in the breeze.

Hear the snake slide everywhere,
Look at the hills above,
But when you see the view,
You'll definitely fall in love.

Come on you people walk along the heath,
Come and smell the flowers,
And watch the tall trees,
Sway in the breeze.

All the birds everywhere,
If you hear the cricket,
You'll be pulling at your hair,
There are no lights on the heath,
That should be very freaky,
But watch out!
There's something being sneaky.

So! Come on all you people,
Walk along the heath!

**Emily Hodges (9)**
**Canford Heath Middle School**

## Dance

Tap, tap, tap,
As the ballerinas prance,
Tap, tap, tap,
As they gracefully dance.

Tap, tap, tap,
As the disco dancers dance,
Tap, tap, tap,
As they practise their stance.

Tap, tap, tap,
Ballroom dancers dance,
Tap, tap, tap,
Followed by the quick step.

Tap, tap, tap,
Lessons have finished,
Tap, tap, tap,
Look forward to next week.

**Emma Turner (10)**
**Canford Heath Middle School**


## My Weird Relatives

My auntie May's got a brain like a sieve,
She forgets where the things in her kitchen all live,
There are plates in the oven and there's jam in a mug,
And loads of carrots squashed in a jug,
My uncle Fred's got ears like cauliflowers,
And listens to conversations for hours and hours,
He can hear from a mile away,
And never gets bored for days and days.

**Nikita Best (9)**
**Canford Heath Middle School**

## Cats And Dogs

Dogs chase balls,
And run into walls,
Cats chase rats,
Into flats.

Cats and dogs,
Run through logs,
Dogs and cats,
Lay on mats.

Cats are fluffy,
Even if they're called Duffy,
Dogs are sweet,
But not very neat.

Dogs and cats,
Are scared of bats,
Cats and dogs,
Don't like frogs.

**Hannah Hickman (9)**
**Canford Heath Middle School**


## I'm A Little Monster!

I'm a little monster that hates to eat peas,
I'm a little monster that likes to eat fleas,
I'm a little monster that hates to eat sweets,
I'm a little monster that likes to eat meats,
I'm a little monster that hates to eat glue,
I'm a little monster that likes to eat *you!*

**Megan Philpott (10)**
**Canford Heath Middle School**

## Weird!

On the island where palm trees grow,
And the island where the monkeys say, 'Bow!'
The elephants say, 'Mow'
On the island where the palm trees grow.

On the island where the giraffes sing,
And the island where the mice say, 'Ping'
The people say, 'Ding-a-ling-ling.'

On the island where the food is pink,
On the island where tigers stink,
The ants' eyes wink,
On the island where the food is pink.

On the island where hippos slurp,
And the island where chameleons burp,
The pigs say, 'Luurrp!'
On the island where hippos burp!

**Laura Cox (9)**
**Canford Heath Middle School**


## Toys!

When a spinning top goes round and round,
It seems that it goes underground,
When the bells go *ding, ding, ding*,
The toys start to sing,
The teddy bears have different colours,
Brown and blue and so many others,
The clowns make a noise,
To all the smelly boys!
Sometimes the dolls go out on a date,
But they're always late.

**Zoë Seabourne (8)**
**Christchurch Junior School**

## Bath Time

It's 7pm on a Monday and there is not a noise in my house,
Except for a tap dripping, going splash in the water,
Then my mum calls, *'Bath time!'*

I start running round in circles thinking of somewhere to hide,
What about the cupboard under the stairs?
Or under the dining room table?
Then it comes to me, *under the bed!*

I crawl under my bed as quickly as I can,
I find my old teddy bear, Cuddles was his name,
Then something black and hairy with eight legs,
It looks like a spider.

*Argh!*

Bubbles in my hair and flannel in my hand,
Oh well, there's always next week.

**Bethan Collingwood (11)**
**Christchurch Junior School**


## School Time

Mum, Mum, it's school time today,
Get out of bed, we might be late,
Come on Mum, into the car,
Come on Mum, it's not that far,
Up the hill and down the lane,
Come on Mum, don't be a pain!
Yes, I'm at school at last,
The time sure did pass,
Oh dear the teachers look like monsters,
I don't want to go to school today Mum.

**Lucy Du Cros (9)**
**Christchurch Junior School**

## Tied With Troubles

'Miss, Miss I can't find my pencil,
My rubber too,
I have nothing to write with,
Oh what am I to do?'

'Miss, Miss my ruler's snapped,
I've forgotten my PE kit,
My scarf, gloves and hat.'

'Mum, Mum, I've spilt my drink,
There's milk on my school clothes,
And it don't half stink.'

'Mum, Mum, I can't find my book,
We've got science tomorrow,
And my homework someone took.'

'Dad, Dad have you seen my glasses?
I can't read my school book,
Without any glasses.'

'Oh I can't find anything.'

'Johnny, have you looked in your schoolbag?'

**Nicole Feeley (10)**
**Christchurch Junior School**


## Animals!

Animals are sometimes funny,
Animals are sometimes clumsy,
Animals are different shapes,
Animals love to race.

Sometimes they are cute and cuddly,
Sometimes they are bad and jumpy,
They are normally very good pets,
But not when it's time to go to the vet's.

**Holly Du Cros (9)**
**Christchurch Junior School**

## The Charge Of The Frog Brigade
*(Based on 'The Charge of The Light Brigade' by Alfred Lord Tennyson)*

Half a leap, half a leap,
Half a leap onward,
Into car valley,
Hopped the six hundred.

'Forward the frog brigade!'
'Ravage their wheels,' he said.
'Get to that pond,' he said.
Onward they hopped.

Cars to the right of them,
Cars to the left of them,
Cars in the front of them,
Revs unnumbered.

Leap over the tarmac road,
Shattered their heavy load,
Into the cool pond! Thanks
To the frog brigade,
Mighty six hundred.

**Kate Wyles (10)**
**Christchurch Junior School**


## Frosty Mornings

The garden lay still under a mantle of white,
Jack Frost had been busy all through the night.
The prettiest sight that I'd ever seen,
Was a view from my window, the old evergreen.
With brilliant red berries, a feast to behold,
For blackbirds and blue tits and robins so bold.
With cobwebs like necklaces, covered with dew,
Like teardrops and diamonds, a magical brew.
Most mornings it's hard to get out of my bed,
Then I hear Mother call, 'Come on sleepyhead!'
I don't want to be late for it's school, I must go,
The weatherman said it's going to snow.

**Eva Cheeseman (10)**
**Christchurch Junior School**

## Foxy, Foxy, Run, Run, Run!

Running through the forest,
My paws soaking wet,
From running through the forest,
In the sweet sunset.

Running through the forest,
Shotguns everywhere,
They're coming to get me, *help!*
Why doesn't anybody care?

Running through the forest,
They're getting nearer,
I can hear the barking, *woof!*
The day is getting clearer.

Running through the forest,
I jump into a hole,
The horses have passed me,
At last, I'm safe, to eat a yummy mole.

**Leanne Faulkner (11)**
**Christchurch Junior School**

## PlayStation

PlayStation's cool, PlayStation's great,
It's something you love or something you hate.
From the time you start to the time you finish,
The love of your game does not diminish.

Fingers on buttons, eyes on the screen,
My facial expressions looking so mean,
My telly sends out visions and sounds,
I drive a car, I fire a gun,
The police are after me, *run, run, run!*

At the beginning, I said it was either love or hate,
But to me the PlayStation's one of my mates.

**Lyam Galpin (11)**
**Christchurch Junior School**

## My Best Friend

My best friend is special,
My best friend is cool,
Whenever I see her,
She's always at my school.

Her mum's a Japanese writer,
Her dad is a cook,
Her brother is a librarian,
Who owns the biggest book.

My best friend is an artist,
My best friend likes to play,
I wish I had more friends like her,
To play with every day.

**Charlotte Lowe (11)**
**Christchurch Junior School**


## My Dance

I love to dance, it makes me smile,
I forget everything for a while.

I bounce and swirl,
My head's in a twirl,
I love to dance, I'm such a girl.

I live to dance, it's so much fun,
I jive and swing under the sun.

I disco and waltz for a while,
I really think you'll love my style.

I love to dance, it makes me smile,
I forget everything for a while.

**Kelly Way (10)**
**Christchurch Junior School**

# The Witches' Spell
*(Based on 'Macbeth')*

Eye of newt and wing of bat,
Snout of pig and magic hat,
Clashing cymbal, beating drum,
Sweeping broom and wizard's thumb.

Stir them up, good and well, then watch
                the smoke go down to hell.

*Double, double, toil and trouble,*
*Fire burn and cauldron bubble.*

Kittens' guts and black of night,
Tadpoles' legs with child's fright,
Wisp of hair, flicker of fire,
Fang of cobra and king's desire.

Watch the cauldron steam and bubble,
Cooking up some fiendish trouble.

*Double, double, toil and trouble,*
*Fire burn and cauldron bubble.*

Bone of goat with golden feather,
Poison bite and frightful weather,
Flash of lightning, welly boot,
Coldest stone and owl's hoot.

In it goes, to the steaming pot, then stir it up, till it's hot.

*Double, double, toil and trouble,*
*Fire burn and cauldron bubble.*

Pinch of sun and cloud of sky,
A foot of bird that can fly,
A mother's voice, a rat's tail,
Scorching water with bread that's stale.

Nasty potion boil and mix,
Then watch us do our magic tricks.

*Double, double, toil and trouble,*
*Fire burn and cauldron bubble.*

Some mouldy toast, baboon's blood,
Ghost's eye and the dirtiest mud,
Vampires' fangs, shred of string,
A black burnt foot with a scorpion sting.

Stir it up nice and thick, then give it to a girl and
Watch her be . . .
*Sick!*

**Bailey Melvin-Teng (10)**
Christchurch Junior School


# Teachers

Our teacher made a kid fall asleep the other day,
Did the teacher notice?
No the kid's still there today.

Our teacher hasn't turned up for ages,
Do you know why?
It was probably me, I gave her two pages of homework.

Our teacher has a really cool car,
How did he manage to afford it?
Teachers must get paid in gold bars.

Our teacher picks his nose,
Where does he put them?
He scrapes them on his clothes.

Our teacher likes school meals,
How does she bare them?
Maybe she likes eels.

Ah but I bet your teacher can't make steam come out of their ears,
OK, you win, you have the worst teacher,
But I have been with this teacher for years,
Who wouldn't go mad having to put up with me for years?

**Jennifer Gee (11)**
Christchurch Junior School

## The Sadness Of The Tsunami (2004)

The joy of Christmas comes again,
The sound of children laughing,
They were having so much fun,
Guess what happened then?

Boxing Day, relaxing on the beach,
Someone swimming in the sea,
The peace was broken, *'Run,'* she screamed,
They could not believe what they could see.

Buildings devastated, people running,
How could this be happening?
Our beautiful country, all our dreams,
Have swept away it seems.

Pictures, photos, where could they be?
How could life be such a misery?
Searching for days for the ones they love,
How could sadness be struck from above?

Muddy grounds, nothing to see,
How could this happen to our country?
The trees have gone, the houses too,
It all came suddenly, out of the blue.

Reunited, we will rebuild,
This cannot destroy our lives,
People from all around the world,
Will *never* let us cry.

**Lauren Burnley (10)**
**Christchurch Junior School**

## Hunting Poems - Fishing

Fish, fish are getting caught,
It's so sad to see them die,
In the Caribbean they are catching fish that fly.

They're being packed up,
And ready to sell,
Attract the people,
Ring the bell.

Crowds of people,
Come and see,
The lovely fish for you.

'Roll up, roll up,'
The fishmonger said,
'£5 a fish,
For you my friend Fred.'

Five o'clock,
Time to pack up,
Poor fish being thrown away,
Fishmongers going to buy new fish to sell,
Why can't he use the ones from today?

**Ellie Lovett (11)**
Christchurch Junior School


## What Do You Collect?

What do you collect?
Books, shells or sharp stones,
Sticks, fossils or old bones?
What do you collect?
Bubbly, smelly old conkers,
Funny, giggly old jokes?

**Samuel Bush (8)**
Christ the King RC Primary School

## Killer Whale Began

He detained the glistening of the sea
And the froth of a boat for his shiny eyes.

He detained the blackness of the sky and
The whiteness of the moon for his coat.

He detained the whiteness of the sharks and
The pointedness from a crocodile's scales and
His teeth were made.

For his fins,
He detained the dorsal fin from a shark and
The pectoral fins of a whale.

For his voice, he detained the screeching of an owl
And the noise of a boat and made his voice.

And killer whale was made.

**Dale Adamson (10)**
**Christ the King RC Primary School**


## Down Behind The Dustbins
*(Based on 'Down Behind the Dustbin' by Michael Rosen)*

Down behind the dustbins,
I met a dog called Rose,
She said, 'Sorry can't play now,
I've got to pose.'

Down behind the dustbins,
I met a dog called Nick,
He said, 'I can't play now,
I've got an itchy tick.'

Down behind the dustbins,
I met a dog called Waggy,
He said, 'Sorry can't play now
Look at me, I'm all raggy.'

**Daisy Lapworth (7)**
**Christ the King RC Primary School**

## Dog Was On The Way . . .

For his eyes he stole the squinting of a newborn baby,
And the weakness of a bush baby.

For his long tongue, he stole the loving of a human,
And the licking of a snake.

For his floppy ears, he stole the squirrel's fluffy tail,
And the softness of a rabbit.

For his black nose, he stole the glittering coal of a warm fire,
And the wetness of the shimmering blue sea.

For his tail, he stole the swaying branches of a
Soft oak tree.

For his furry black coat, he stole the night sky,
Black skin and the star's bright effect.

**Jordan Bell (11)**
**Christ the King RC Primary School**


## Down Behind The Dustbins
*(Based on 'Down Behind the Dustbin' by Michael Rosen)*

Down behind the dustbins,
I met a dog called Meg,
She said, 'I cannot play now,
I have to hang my coat up on my peg.'

Down behind the dustbins,
I met a dog called Sam,
He said, 'I cannot play now
I have to feed myself with some ham.'

Down behind the dustbins,
I met a dog called Pose,
She said, 'I cannot play now,
I need to smell a rose.'

**Megan Rose Davis (7)**
**Christ the King RC Primary School**

## Dolphin Dreams

She took the rippling of the ocean
And the hand of the seabed
To make her skin.

She took the mistiness of the moon
And the glinting of the stars
To make her eyes.

She took the eagle's voice that took watch
And the whistle of the wind
To make her song.

She took the palms of the trees
And the petals of the flowers
To make her tail.

She took the opening of the sand
And the curl of the shells
To make her bottle-nose.

Finally, she took the heart of the world,
Mixed together with her love
To make her personality.

She had succeeded.

**Megan Barrington (10)**
**Christ the King RC Primary School**


## Down Behind The Dustbin
*(Based on 'Down Behind the Dustbin' by Michael Rosen)*

Down behind the dustbin,
I met a dog called Flower,
She said, 'Sorry got to go,
And get more powers.'

Down behind the dustbin,
I met a dog called Drink,
He said, 'Sorry got to go to
The toilet because I'm turning pink.'

**Shelby Fiorentini (8)**
**Christ the King RC Primary School**

## The Rabbit!

She took the shimmering water,
She took the pinkness of a marshmallow,
To make the lovely pink, wet button nose.

She took the whiteness of the candyfloss,
She took the fluffiness of a pillow,
To make her tail.

She took the floppiness of a certain curtain,
She took the pinkness from a flamingo,
To make her ears.

She took the blueness from the deepest sea,
She took the sparkles from the most magical lake,
To make her eyes.

She took the hop from a grasshopper,
To make her leap.

She took the fluffiness from the clouds,
She took the purity from the snow,
To make her furry coat.

And Rabbit was created.

**Mercedes Apps (10)**
**Christ the King RC Primary School**


## Down Behind The Dustbins
*(Based on 'Down Behind the Dustbin' by Michael Rosen)*

Down behind the dustbins,
I met a dog called Sam,
He said, 'Sorry can't play now,
I've got to eat my ham!'

Down behind the dustbins,
I met a dog called Sam,
He said, 'Sorry can't play now,
I have to eat my lamb!'

**Alisha Aragones (8)**
**Christ the King RC Primary School**

## What Do You Collect?

What do you collect?
What do you collect?
Bells, shells, plants,
Drums, boxes, ants?

What do you collect?
Ants, bait, snails,
Nuts, bars, nails?

What do you collect?
Trucks, newspapers, thunder,
Vests, oak trees, underwear?

What do you collect?
Seeds, leads, tellies,
Buses, blinds, jelly?

What do you collect?
Toadstools, chairs, bears,
Stairs, Mars bars, stairs?

**Callum Cooper (8)**
**Christ the King RC Primary School**


## Down Behind The Dustbins
*(Based on 'Down Behind the Dustbin' by Michael Rosen)*

Down behind the dustbins,
I met a dog called Shoala,
She said, 'Sorry, need to go
And get my toy polar!'

Down behind the dustbins,
I met a dog called Nurse,
She said, 'I need to go now
And try to find my purse.'

**Christina Murphy (8)**
**Christ the King RC Primary School**

## Gerbil's Origin

Gerbil was born,
For his fur,
He grabbed the coat of a phoenix,
And the darkness of the night sky.

He grabbed the sharpness of the chainsaw,
He grabbed the poison of a witch's wart,
For his claws.

At dawn,
He grabbed the swiftness of the shadows,
And the slyness of a cat and the flowing
Of water for his walk.

He grabbed the fear of a mouse,
The whiteness of a glass window
For his bite.

For his spirit,
He grabbed the toughness of an elephant,
He took the braveness of a lion,
And Gerbil was perfected.

**Joshua Manzi (11)**
**Christ the King RC Primary School**


## My Favourite Things
*(Inspired by 'The Sound of Music')*

Chicken korma curry and my PS2,
Spaghetti Bolognese and my cool nephew,
Colourful parrots with multicoloured wings,
These are a few of my favourite things.

Liverpool Football Club and pepperoni pizza,
Tenerife and my mum and all of my friends,
Colourful balloons with strange-looking strings,
These are a few of my favourite things.

**Anthony Grieve (10)**
**Christ the King RC Primary School**

## Dog Was Being Created!

Dog was being created.

For his tail,
He took the moving of the branches,
He took the silkiness from curtains,
And his tail was created.

For his ears,
He took the pinkness of a flamingo,
He took the fluffiness of a rabbit,
And his ears were created.

For his eyes,
He took the sparkling of a sparkle pen,
He took the blueness of the ocean,
And his eyes were created.

For his teeth,
He took the whiteness of milk,
He took the sharpness of pins,
And his teeth were created.

For his voice,
He took the loudness of thunder,
He took the howling of a wolf,
And his voice was created.

Then that night for his nose,
He took the blackness of the sky,
He took the wetness of a puddle.

And dog was created!

**Ryan Hoff (11)**
**Christ the King RC Primary School**

## This Is The Beginning Of The Snake

To make Snake's eyes,
He took the blackness of the night
And the glittering stars.
It was a wonderful sight.

To make Snake's hiss,
He stole the howling of the wind
And the whistling of the kettle.
His voice was settled.

To make Snake's fangs,
He seized a poisonous venom
And a sharp knife
To make trouble and strife.

To make Snake's scales,
He took the redness of fire
And the softness of silk.
It was all to his desire.

To make Snake's tongue,
He seized the strength of a buffalo
And the shape of the letter Y.
As he hissed it pointed to the sky.

To make Snake's movement,
He stole the wriggle of a worm
And the swish of a fish's tail.
Snake was formed.

**Joanna Treggiden (10)**
**Christ the King RC Primary School**

## My Anaconda

His hiss was as loud as a lion's roar,
He was as long as two buses put together,
His teeth were so pointy, he could bite through anything.
His skin was as smooth as plastic.

His beady eyes were as dark as grapes,
And as shiny as marbles,
His forked tongue looked like the letter Y.

His poison was like a deadly nightshade,
His scales, he scraped the scales from a mermaid,
Lying on the sand.

**Oliver Moyse (10)**
**Christ the King RC Primary School**


## Lion Cub

He takes the love from a kitten,
A heart from a child,
The fierceness of his dad.
His personality is made.

He takes the howling from the wolf,
And the echo of the valley.
His voice is made.

He takes the softness from silk
And he takes the spots from the leopard in the snow.
His skin is made.

He takes the marbles from the marble jar
And the glitter from Heaven above
That fills his eyes with love.

My cub is made.

**Shelby Richardson (11)**
**Christ the King RC Primary School**

## The Tiger Cub

He took the gleam of the wolf,
The darkness of the Devil,
The style of a cat
For his eyes.

He took the playfulness of a puppy,
And the love of a child
And made his personality.

He took the echo of the valley
And the howling of a wolf
And his voice was made.

He stole the coat from an adult tiger
And finally the loveable tiger cub was made.

**Kelly-Marie Dady (11)**
Christ the King RC Primary School


## Leopard's Arriving

For his spots he gathered the light of the ancient stars
And the darkness of the gloomy caves.

For his roar he gathered the thumping of the wild jungle
And the rumbling of the smoky factories.

For his speed he gathered the dash of a hundred cars
And the whizz of the stampeding wildebeests.

For his eyes he gathered the glistening of an emerald
And the shining of gold.

For his tail he gathered the swiftness of a bullet
And the strength of an elephant's tusks.

For his nose he gathered the wetness of a flowing stream
And the skill of a sly hunter.

Leopard arrived!

**Liam Giffin (11)**
Christ the King RC Primary School

## Favourite Things
*(Inspired by 'The Sound of Music')*

Fluffy cats and pretty little flowers,
Cute little bats and Bruce Almighty with powers.
Diamonds and rubies and sparkling rings,
These are a few of my favourite things.

Mrs Clark and all my friends,
Dogs that bark and toys that my dad mends.
Dancing and prancing as I sing,
These are a few of my favourite things.

In bed I watch DVDs,
My favourite colour is red, boiling hot macaroni cheese.
Pretty birds with bright coloured wings,
These are a few of my favourite things.

Playing tennis and having fun,
With my uncle Dennis we like to run.
He brought me a balloon with multicoloured string,
These are a few of my favourite things.

**Rebecca Watts (10)**
**Christ the King RC Primary School**


## How To Make A Snake

For its hiss
It seized the movement of the tide going in
And out, flowing on the sandy bay.

It seized the colour of a glistening ruby,
It seized the shape of a fork for its tongue.

It seized the dark green stain from a pike's back,
It seized the sleekness of a silver coin for its scales.

It seized the pounce of a tiger,
It seized the slithering of a king cobra.

It seized the shape of a marble,
It seized the blue star for its beady eyes
And the snake was born.

**Jack Whitton (10)**
**Christ the King RC Primary School**

## The Big Snake

The snake is coming . . .

For his skin
He seizes the strength of a dragon's scales,
He seizes the green of the grass,
His skin was made.

For his eyes
He seizes the black of a marble,
He seizes the yellow of the sun for his pupils,
His eyes were made.

For his tail
He seizes the strength of a dinosaur's tail,
He seizes the rattling of a rattlesnake,
His tail was made.

For his teeth
He seizes the venom of all the snakes in the world,
He seizes the strength of a lion's tooth,
His teeth were made.

For his tongue
He seizes the sharpness of a knife,
He seizes the loudness of a plane for his hiss,
His tongue was made.

The snake is here.

**Alexander Reeves (10)**
**Christ the King RC Primary School**


## Fear

It sounds like a ghost wailing,
It smells like revenge,
It feels like goosebumps running up your arm.
It's the colour of fresh blood,
It tastes like fire,
It looks like a vampire enjoying the taste of blood.

**David Cherrett (10)**
**Christ the King RC Primary School**

## My Favourite Things
*(Inspired by 'The Sound of Music')*

Playing on my computer and on my Game Boy,
Eating red strawberries and playing with toys,
In choir with Mrs Fisher where we all sing,
These are a few of my favourite things.

When I go to see Southampton with my dad and mum,
I have a big burger that fills up my tum,
My best friend has a parrot with multicoloured wings,
These are a few of my favourite things.

Harry Potter and when he does magic,
If Ron Weasley died it would be tragic,
When you get married you get a diamond ring,
These are a few of my favourite things.

My DVD player and my cousin Jemma,
I like playing tennis with my grampy Denis,
Elvis Presley's songs make him the king,
These are a few of my favourite things.

**Gabrielle Excell (10)**
Christ the King RC Primary School


## My Favourite Things
*(Inspired by 'The Sound of Music')*

I love to read my books,
I spend a lot of time on my looks,
I spend every night looking at the stars,
A balloon with a strong string,
These are a few of my favourite things.

I like to eat apples,
I go to chapels,
My necklace always blings,
These are a few of my favourite things.

**Sarah Comerford (9)**
Christ the King RC Primary School

## My Favourite Things
*(Inspired by 'The Sound of Music')*

Harry Potter movies and spicy, hot rice,
A scrummy fruit salad and drink cold as ice,
Gigantic big presents wrapped up in string,
These are a few of my favourite things.

Cute fluffy kittens and sweet smelling flowers,
Multicoloured butterflies and cold, refreshing showers,
In our music lesson, with the bells that ring,
These are a few of my favourite things.

Flaming hot chicken, lemonade and lime,
Beautiful rainbows and warm sunshine,
With the choir that love to sing,
These are a few of my favourite things.

Fun and games are lots of fun,
Football and netball, I love to run,
At the end of the day when the school bell rings,
These are a few of my favourite things.

**Sophie Robinson (9)**
**Christ the King RC Primary School**


## My Favourite Things
*(Inspired by 'The Sound of Music')*

The raindrop falling onto a flower,
The brave Superman without any power,
With rainbow-coloured string,
These are a few of my favourite things.

The beautiful Bratz in the mall,
Yasmin and Chloe get a call,
The sound of the ring, ring,
These are a few of my favourite things.

**Sophie Batty (10)**
**Christ the King RC Primary School**

## These Are A Few Of My Favourite Things
*(Inspired by 'The Sound of Music')*

They're cool things, they're Bratz,
Soft and cute, it's my cat,
I love spring,
These are a few of my favourite things.

Shiny icy snowflakes,
My mum, she's the best at baking,
I love dime rings,
These are a few of my favourite things.

I love ice cream,
I have beautiful dreams,
I like chicken wings,
These are a few of my favourite things.

**Nicole Allen (9)**
Christ the King RC Primary School

## My Favourite Things
*(Inspired by 'The Sound of Music')*

Watching DVDs with macaroni cheese,
Playing my Game Boy, good people say please,
I like pizza with chicken wings,
These are a few of my favourite things.

I play on my Xbox but I am in the mood for a curry,
The takeaway is closing soon so I better hurry,
All of my presents are tied with sparkly string,
These are a few of my favourite things.

On a dull day I play with my cat
And in the evening he has a snack.
When I'm bored I love to sing,
These are a few of my favourite things.

**Carlos Aragones (10)**
Christ the King RC Primary School

## My Favourite Things
*(Inspired by 'The Sound of Music')*

Lovely prawn crackers
But I call them mackers,
Arsenal invincibles
But not yet big syllables,
The taste of KFC chicken wings,
These are a few of my favourite things.

Speedy bike riding
With my sister hiding,
The Millennium Stadium cheering,
The cars that are steering,
Also the warm start of spring,
These are a few of my favourite things.

Exciting DVDs,
Tomato sauce on peas,
Great country, Wales
And all the sales,
Christmas bells ting,
These are a few of my favourite things.

**Micky Edwards (10)**
**Christ the King RC Primary School**


## Frustration Is . . .

When your sister is on your Game Boy,
A teacher when the children don't listen,
Like an animal trapped in a zoo,
Like a plant dead in a pot,
Like a dog growling.
It's like a cat killing a mouse,
Like a fish not biting when you're fishing,
Like a fish in a tank.

**Robert Herbert (9)**
**Christ the King RC Primary School**

## My Favourite Things
*(Inspired by 'The Sound of Music')*

The slush of me skiing the coastline of Devon,
Climbing up high on a cool expedition.
The tweeting of budgies as they flap their own wings,
These are a few of my favourite things.

I like my mum's pizza with slices of ham,
Playing with my friend, his name is Sam.
Walking in the countryside, worshipping kings,
These are a few of my favourite things.

**Marco Bolt (10)**
Christ the King RC Primary School

## Summer

Summer is like the taste of chocolate ice cream,
Summer feels like a ball of fire raging towards you,
Summer sounds like your heart beating as the sun goes down,
Summer is the colour of a gold brick,
Summer is the smell of melting chocolate,
Summer looks like the salty sea tumbling
Towards you on the crispy sand.

**Francesca Young (9)**
Christ the King RC Primary School

## Happiness

Happiness smells like a rose in a forest,
Happiness tastes like sweet strawberries,
It looks like a bright rainbow near a lake,
It feels like a fluffy kitten in my arms,
It looks like shining stars up in space.

**Lucy Field (10)**
Christ the King RC Primary School

## Down Behind The Dustbins
*(Based on 'Down Behind the Dustbin' by Michael Rosen)*

Down behind the dustbins
I met a dog called Jake.
He said, 'Sorry I can't stay
I have to go and bake.'

Down behind the dustbins
I met a dog called Melly.
She said, 'Sorry I have to go,
I need to go and fill my belly.'

Down behind the dustbins
I met a dog called Sam.
He said, 'Sorry I have to go,
I need to feed my lamb.'

**Jenna Cornick (8)**
**Christ the King RC Primary School**


## Favourite Things
*(Inspired by 'The Sound of Music')*

Beautiful flowers and small fluffy cats,
Going round my friend's house
And playing with Bratz.
Playing at Christmas while sleigh bells ring,
These are a few of my favourite things.

I do dances, that's where I do my prances,
Strawberry and berry and lots of juicy cherries,
DVDs and Man United sweets,
These are a few of my favourite things.

**Melissa Biddlecombe (9)**
**Christ the King RC Primary School**

## My Favourite Things
*(Inspired by 'The Sound of Music')*

Whiskers on rabbits with soft furry hair,
Bratz with cats and a cuddly teddy bear.
Noisy parrots with bright coloured wings,
These are a few of my favourite things.

Ice cream so frosty like snowflakes that stay
On my nose and eyelashes.
Ice-cold white winter, please tune into spring,
These are a few of my favourite things.

**Poppy Brock (9)**
**Christ the King RC Primary School**


## Darkness And Light

Darkness is the sound of the fridge humming.
Light is the sound of the birds singing like the voice of
                                        Charlotte Church.
Darkness feels like my mum shouting.
Light feels like a chocolate bar melting and dipped in steaming
                                        hot chocolate.
The colour of darkness is like a haunted house or the
                                        'Goosebumps' series.
The colour of light is like ice cream melting in the boiling sun.

**David Long (9)**
**Christ the King RC Primary School**


## A Fun School

I go to school and do my sums,
I always play with my funky chums.
I really love doing art,
I'm very, very, very smart.
We're really good at maths and science,
We never pay our car alliance.

**Andrew Manston (9)**
**Hillbourne Middle School**

## The Minibeast

I like to look at a minibeast,
Nothing is better in the least.
I like looking at a bat,
When it lies flat on a mat.
I also like to look at a cat,
When it's quickly catching a rat.
I want to look at a skeleton,
Or a scaly green Martian.
I would also like to see a ghost
Who looks like a scary host.
I really hope that everyone
Will also think they're lots of fun.
When it's time for them to go,
I definitely know.
It's time for them to go away,
For us to see another day.

**Thomas Lovell (8)**
**Hillbourne Middle School**


## A Tropical Island

The sun arose with a giant smile on his bright yellow face.
The palm trees yawned at the wake-up call of the parachuting
                                                                                    coconuts.
As the deep blue sea gave the rocks and pebbles a ride
The banana trees giggled with joy.
It was sunset and the sun had to go, leaving the moon as king of
                                                                                   the night sky.
Stars began to appear and blink with happiness as the island's
Nature was mesmerised in amazement.
All was calm as the coconuts, bananas and leaves swayed in a
                                                                                    deep sleep.
The moon smiled with joy at the peaceful island's rough skin.

**Ryan Copleston (11)**
**Hillbourne Middle School**

## Ten Cool Children

Ten cool children, playing in the school,
But two went off to the swimming pool.
So there were only eight cool children playing in the school.

Eight cool children dreaming they can fly,
But two went off to look at the sky.
So there were only six cool children dreaming they can fly.

Six cool children doing PE,
But two went off to see Poole quay.
So there were only four cool children doing PE.

Four cool children having fun,
But two went off to learn how to run.
So there were only two cool children having fun.

Two cool children dressing up in black,
But then everybody else came back.

**Holly Grant & Adam Wood (9)**
**Hillbourne Middle School**


## Yuck

My mum said we must eat healthily.
When we sit down for our tea
I want cakes, crisps and a strawberry shake.

But that is not what my mum will really make.

Sprouts are poison balls,
Cabbage is a killer.

Mum said they're a healthy filler
And I said . . . 'Yuck!'

**Kiarna Ducker (11)**
**Hillbourne Middle School**

## Henry And His Wife Jane

'What would you like Henry darling, would it be a baby girl called Mary.'
*'No,* I just want a boy!'
'Are you sure you don't want a girl, because we can call her anything you like?'
*'No,* I just want a boy!'
'We can have her for your birthday trip.'
*'No,* I just want a boy!'
'She could sleep in my room, she won't give you any trouble.'
*'No,* I said just a boy!'
'You can choose what she wears and you won't have to pay for any of the clothes.'
*'No,* just a boy!'
'You don't have to feed her because I will do things like that.'
*'No,* I said just a baby boy!'

9 months later . . .

A boy so cherished, he did arrive!
So Henry, so thankful was he.
He said to his wife I'm so pleased with life,
I'm really filled with glee.

**Jordan Witt (9)**
**Hillbourne Middle School**


## Every Day

We never sleep, we never peep.
We never talk, we never walk.
We're never mean, we're never lean.
We never fall, we do play ball.
We are so cool, the boys all drool.
We all do rhyme and we all climb.
We are all smart, we all like art.
We all use pens, we all build dens.

**Jade Davis (8)**
**Hillbourne Middle School**

## The Seasons

*Spring*
Spring is a time when things are born,
Farmers plant their wheat and corn.
Buds begin to swell and grow,
The sun's face begins to glow.

*Summer*
Summer's here, the birds are singing,
Lots of people are going swimming.
Children playing on the sand,
Mums and dads listen to the band.

*Autumn*
Autumn leaves are falling down,
They make a blanket on the ground.
All the conkers on the tree,
With their coats as spiky as can be.

*Winter*
Winter's snow is on its way,
Dress up warm and go out to play.
The days are short, the nights are long,
We can't wait for spring to come along.

**Daniel Winwood (10)**
**Hillbourne Middle School**


## Dogs

Dogs are cute and very fluffy,
Dogs are soft and can be puffy.

Dogs eat lots and walk on leads,
Dogs have beds, that's what they need.

Dogs can be nice or a bit mean,
Dogs can be evil or very clean.

Dogs are kind and go back home,
Dogs like people and chew a bone.

**Hannah Whatley (9)**
**Hillbourne Middle School**

## Goodbye Mum And Dad

Goodbye Mum and Dad,
I'm going to university.
Goodbye Mum and Dad,
Don't worry you will still see me.

Don't worry or cry,
For now it's only goodbye,
Think of all the peace and quiet,
For I won't be there to run riot.

I'll think about you every day,
But soon you'll be thinking thank goodness she's gone away.
I promise I'll do my best,
When it is time for a very hard test.

Don't worry you'll see me soon,
When I come home at the end of June!

**Rachel Lye (10)**
**Hillbourne Middle School**


## Every Day

We never sleep,
We never peep.
We never talk,
We never walk.
We're never mean,
We're never lean.
We never fall,
The boys all drool.
We all do rhyme
And we all climb.
We are all smart,
We all like art.
We all use pens,
We all build dens.

**Scarlett Adams (9)**
**Hillbourne Middle School**

## Make Animals

Now the potion will begin, chicken's beak and fish's fin,
Eye of newt and tongue of frog, mix together, make a dog.
Rabbit's foot and kitten's hair, chuck them in and make a bear,
Horse's leg and fox's tail, stir it quick and make a whale.
Tiger's stripe and lion's roar, and conjure up a wild boar,
Wart of toad and penguin's wing, mix it in and make something.
Stir it round and stir it through, but be cautious as you do,
Now it is nearly done, so add a worm just for fun.

**Katie Bligh (10)**
**Hillbourne Middle School**


## It's A . . .

Massive mane,
Gives pain,
Fast mover,
Land groover,
Jungle hider,
On land glider,
Large body,
Annoys everybody,
It's a . . .

**Thomas Holden (10)**
**Hillbourne Middle School**


## School Days

I go to school and do my work,
I go in the playground and always smirk.

I do my maths and add up sums,
Then I hang out with my chums.

I really love doing art,
I am very, very smart.

**Lydia Proudley & Melissa Buckland (9)**
**Hillbourne Middle School**

## At Tesco's

'Hello, welcome to Tesco's, what would you like?'
'Just a magazine please.'
'Any fruit, vegetables or chicken pies?'
'No, just a magazine please.'
'Any CDs, DVDs or videos if you please?'
'No, just a magazine please.'
'Would you like a pencil sir or a box of toys?'
*'No! Just a magazine please!'*
'Sorry we are out of stock.'

**Connor Dyke (9)**
**Hillbourne Middle School**


## Animals

Animals can be short or tall,
They may like to scamper or crawl.
They're colourful and amazing creatures,
They might have ugly or beautiful features.
These animals could be birds, fish or cats,
Or even dogs, hens or rats.

**Olivia Coles (9)**
**Hillbourne Middle School**


## Think!

Oh think about the world ahead,
As there are many paths to tread,
Think about all those lives gone to death,
Why did these disasters take away their breath?
Think about the Asian disaster . . . the tsunami,
Bet they're jealous of you and me.
Hey, we might not even wake up tomorrow,
So why lay in all this sorrow,
Just grab a cold, refreshing drink,
Then look up into the sky and *think!*

**Joseph Benham (10)**
**Hillbourne Middle School**

## King Henry

'I want to behead my second wife.'
'Why would you do that?'
'Why shouldn't I do that?'
'She's beautiful and graceful.'
'But also very hateful, she gave me a child,
But it was a girl.'
'A girl, what's wrong with a girl?'
'I'll tell you what's wrong with a girl!
I want a boy to take over from me,
I mean think of all the things a girl can do,
Make-up here, make-up there,
Make-up everywhere.'
'I see, I can't change your mind?'
'Yes that's right, so do you mind,
I have to go and tell my wife she has
A date with the executioner.'

**Aimee Auger (9)**
**Hillbourne Middle School**


## Anger

Anger is red,
It smells like burnt toast.
Anger tastes like burnt chips,
It looks like a volcano erupting.
Anger is in Hell.

Anger is black,
It smells of smoke.
Anger tastes like burnt food,
It looks like you're going to explode.
Anger is evil.

**Jordan Bromley (10)**
**Hillbourne Middle School**

## At The Supermarket

'Hello, how are you? What would you like?'
'A box of chocolates please.'
'How about some bread or fish fingers from Fred?'
'A box of chocolates please.'
'A piece of steak or chocolate cake?'
'A box of chocolates please.'
'A pizza with cheese or frosty peas?'
'A box of chocolates.'
'Have you checked aisle three? And did you say please?'
*'I said, a box of chocolates, please!'*
'So you did say please, did you want cheese?'
*'No, just chocolates!'*
'OK, here you go, just go and pay Mo.'
*'Oh no!'*

**Thomas Legg (10)**
**Hillbourne Middle School**


## Summer Days

Summer days lazing in the sun,
Summer days they've only just begun.
Summer days having lots of fun!
Summer days dancing in the sun.

Playing in the sand,
Playing in the sea,
What a great day,
Come out and play.

Summer days lazing in the sun,
Summer days they've only just begun.
Summer days having lots of fun!
Summer days dancing in the sun.

**Jade Fudge (11)**
**Hillbourne Middle School**

## Ten Cool Kids

Ten cool kids
Hanging about,
Two got bored
And eight fell out.

Eight cool kids
Having a fight,
Two made friends
And six made a kite.

Six cool kids
Chilling in the park,
Two ran away
And four heard a bark.

Four cool kids
Playing with a dog,
Two threw a stick
And two chased a frog.

Two cool kids
Playing in the trees,
One went home
And hurt his knee.

Ten cool kids
All having fun,
Playtime's over
This rhyme is done.

**Abbie McKenna (9)**
**Hillbourne Middle School**


## The Greatest Skipper

I am the greatest ever seen,
I never tumble, ne'er lean.
I skip at night, I skip all day,
I never stop to eat or play.

**Ashleigh Phillips (9)**
**Hillbourne Middle School**

## Remembrance Day

War is as black as night, cold as death,
Stealing lives like a theft,
Man killing man, bad or good,
As the living fight, the dead lie still as wood,
Why did Hitler have to strike?
Changing things to what he would like,
Peace it seems, will never come,
Though only bombs and guns making people glum,
Finally the war has ended, bodies lying all around,
As I walk among the dead, people search the ground,
My eyes like eagles, searching for
My very own grandpa, will he be lying on the floor?
And now it's only a month from the war,
Oh why did people think they would score?
And where a soldier would have fought
Now grows a poppy full of love, grief and thought,
And poppies are as red as blood,
As grievers cry a salty flood,
Each poppy, each soul, grows very high,
I've given my story and why,
To stop the wars,
Even the winner will see many bodies on many floors.

**Eleanor Pickford (9)**
**Hillbourne Middle School**


## Hope

Hope to me is pink,
It is a pretty colour.

Hope smells like raspberry juice,
It tastes sweet and tangy.

It is like the fresh air and the bright sun
That hangs in the sky.

Hope feels smooth and soft,
Hope lives in the centre of our hearts.

**Natasha Carter (9)**
**Hillbourne Middle School**

## The Monster Snooze

Can I hear a piglet snorting?
Is the donkey braying loud?
Is the kettle overheating?
Can I hear a rioting crowd?

Is the traffic bearing down?
Is the lion at a roar?
Are the Harpies in a moan?
Can I hear an aircraft soar?

No, the noise is much too even,
Sometimes soft and sometimes loud.
Like a saw, it's rough when cleaving,
Sometimes wild but often proud.

This cave is damp and dark and clammy,
I touch the walls, they sweat and ooze.
Although asleep he's still quite scary,
The noise? It's just the monster's snooze!

**Fleur Yeats (10)**
**Hillbourne Middle School**


## A Poem For Witches Like Me

Hubble, bubble, boil and trouble,
A potion I shall make using the blood of a snake.

Eye of cat, toe of rat,
Tail of mouse, tongue of louse.
Wing of bird with lemon curd,
Whisker of rabbit brings a bad habit.
Fin of fish won't give you a wish,
Honey from a bear becomes your worst nightmare,
For I shall have a potion.

A sniff of my potion and you will need skin lotion,
Bring close to your lip and take a small sip.
Now get ready for fright, dark in the night,
So now you've been warned - beware of witches like me.

**Jessica Longstaff (11)**
**Hillbourne Middle School**

## Red Nose Day

Red Nose Day,
What can that be?
I have been told
It's to raise money
For the poor families.

Poor families,
What can they be?
It's families a bit
Like you and me!

You and me,
What can that be?
People everywhere
And Third World countries
We hear about on TV!

Red Nose Day,
What can that mean?
We need to raise money
To help people less
Fortunate than me!

**Michael Sneddon (11)**
**Hillbourne Middle School**


## My Garden

M other birds feeding their baby chicks,
Y oung fawns jumping around.

G olden sunshine all around,
A pples falling from apple trees,
R abbits hopping around the green grass,
D aisies blowing in the cool breeze,
E verlasting colours,
N ew animals being born every day.

**Lauren Belben (9)**
**Hillbourne Middle School**

## The Colourful Lizard

I'm an enormous lizard
With colourful skin
Who jumps around
Like a brand new pin.
I am definitely the most
Colourful thing in the forest.

**Tanvir Ahmed & Chris Gloster (9)**
Hillbourne Middle School


## Love

Love is pink, soft, gentle and happy.
Love is when you stay in on a Saturday with family.
Love is being loved by family or friends.
Love smells like a red rose in summer.
Love is a wonderful feeling.
Love feels like a radiant summer's day.
Love feels like lying on a soft pillow.
Love is the best feeling in the world.
You know if you're in love because it's a true feeling.

**Sarah Benfield (10)**
Hillbourne Middle School


## Sneaky Snake

I am a snake all green and grey,
Who likes to go outside to play,
And when I see a running mouse,
I take him right back to my house.

**Tia Druce (8) & Charlie Triggs (9)**
Hillbourne Middle School

## Ten Little Pins

Ten little pins
Sitting on the wall,
One went bang,
One went small,
One went pop,
One flew away,
One went home,
One had to stay,
Two went off in a car,
Two went driving in a racing car,
One went shopping,
One went to school,
Now there's no more
Pins sitting on the wall.

**Jessica Nash (8) & Philippe Lord (9)**
**Hillbourne Middle School**


## The Skipping Girl

I never slide, I never slip,
I skip and jump but never trip.
When I'm on my skipping ropes,
I can skip down massive slopes.
If I get tied up at all,
I always stop and never fall.
When I'm skipping down the road,
I scare away the little toads.
When I go to bed at night,
I won't skip till dawn's first light.
I dream about it in my dreams,
I'm always skipping by the streams.

**Rebekah Kerr (8) & Maxine Wilson (9)**
**Hillbourne Middle School**

## Sitting Here

I'm so bored, I hate sitting here,
Sometimes I wish I could walk down the pier!

Even though I'm not keen on walking,
I just can't stand sitting and talking!

Maybe I could ask to go to the quay,
We could get some chips, go on a shopping spree.

I'm ever so bored, I hate sitting here,
Sometimes I wish I could fly somewhere.

Even though it's planes I fear,
*I just can't stand sitting here!*

**Sophie Allisett (10)**
Hillbourne Middle School

## The Sphinx Of Ancient Egypt

Head of a human and the body of a lion,
Has the Sphinx of ancient Egypt.
Mystery lies within the sandy body
Of the Sphinx of ancient Egypt.

It has stood here for hundreds of years,
A mighty statue, behold.
It stands and stares straight ahead,
Resting peacefully in the scorching golden sand.

It guards the mighty pyramids
And a secret riddle it hides.
Maybe it hides a royal treasure,
Full of silver and gold.

The mighty Sphinx has been standing for thousands of years,
But how many more years will it be standing?
How many more years will it guard the pyramids?
How many more years will it be there?

**Danielle Wickham (9)**
Port Regis School

## Today I Feel

Today I feel . . .
As gloomy as a fraying, forgotten glove,
Cross as a raging bull,
Small as a tiny mouse,
Sad as a brown rotting berry,
Glum as a blunt, unused needle,
Cold as a frosty, icy winter,
As sad as a fireless dragon.

Today I feel . . .
Sweet as a fresh rosebud,
Excited as a spotted, pouncing cheetah cub,
Cool as a fresh green cucumber,
As eager as a golden eagle,
Fit as a beautiful lion,
Hot as a red chilli pepper,
And that is how I feel today.

**Sophie Geikie-Cobb (7)**
**Port Regis School**


## Nine Things In A Magic Candy Store Owner's Bag

Nine things found in a magic candy store owner's bag . . .

Fizzy crackle candy, which tingles in your mouth,
Vitamins which actually taste good,
A wallet full of money worth lots of boxes of sweets.

Chewy little sweets, strawberry flavour,
A pen with ink that smells so good you can almost taste it,
Sour spray which disintegrates on your tongue.

Mints which work like helium,
Bubblegum already blown with everlasting flavour
And peanut butter fudge which never expires.

**Halimah Schmidt (10)**
**Port Regis School**

## Hidden Danger

Have you ever seen a snake?
I have.
The feeling inside me
Showed in the look on my face.

It was a water snake,
Long and scaly
And terrifying.

It was sunbathing on a rock,
It moved its head from side to side
Licked its lips
And wondered what we were doing.

Have you ever seen a snake
In the wild?
I hadn't 'til now.

When I came back a few minutes later
All I saw was the swish of a tail,
And it had gone.

**Anastasia Mackaness (9)**
**Port Regis School**


## An Oak Tree Branch

Crinkly leaves that you can feel with fingertips,
Smells like a freshly cut Christmas tree,
The acorns are smooth like a wooden floor,
Buzzing with life,
Some acorns fresh, some not,
Bugs creeping round the leaves,
The leaves dotted yellow,
Soon the acorn will die and regrow next year.

**Freddie Ball (10)**
**Port Regis School**

## A Crag Of Beauty

Enclosed by beauty,
Rocky crags shaped like sharks' teeth
Silhouetted against the clear blue sky.
It is stunning!
Snow caught up in crevices and gullies.
Water captured frozen as it cascades down the granite walls.
The frozen water is like a veil over the mountain.
Footprints in the snow reveal nature's secret multitude
Surviving in the harsh climate.
Trees appear lower down the valley where nature hides.
The sun glares down on the glistening snow.

It is the picturesque scene of the
*Mountains.*

**Hannah Bonnell (11)**
**Port Regis School**


## Seven Things You Might Find In An Old Witch's Pocket

A rotting skull full of cobwebs and spiders,
A boiling cauldron with all sorts of nasty, disgusting things inside.
A jar with all the ingredients for her magical potions,
An amazing wand that could turn people into frogs,
A pot full of irresistible poisonous candies that nobody could
                                                                stop eating,
A wicked broom so that she could ride around in the sky,
Finally her pet Basilisk with dangerous, gleaming yellow eyes
That would kill anyone who looked directly into them.

**Nicholas Evans (10)**
**Port Regis School**

## The Bouncer Race

The race begins at the top of the driveway,
My mum and my aunt
On two bright orange bouncers!

With a good push on the ground,
They're off!

The laughing, the bouncing, the jumping,
The thump of feet landing
Then springing off again.
Hair flying everywhere.
Both racers trying hard to overtake
But not fall off.

We're all together
Playing games
Laughing and having a good time

The race finishes
It's close . . . but . . .

My aunt just wins!

**Emily Watts (10)**
**Port Regis School**


## The Statue Of Nelson

High up in the sky
Looking down on everyone,
Superior among others
He watches with his one eye,
On his thin but huge pillar
Carved from the finest stone
Just for him.
The sun shines proudly on the great
Admiral Horatio Nelson.

**Harry Waddington (10)**
**Port Regis School**

## Ten Things In Peter Pan's Hideout

I once went to Never Land,
I was lost underground,
Then I saw Peter's den
And this is what I found . . .

A small box of fairy dust,
A fold up sandy floor,
Books and books of fairy tales
And there's more.

Some sort of clay pipe,
A medicine bottle,
Twelve straw beds.

Chubby cheeked children round a giant table,
A feast of make-believe food
A memory of a victorious fight,
A hero brave and good.

I never found my way back
To Never Land,
It's
Forever Never Land.

**Ella Spottiswood (11)**
Port Regis School


## A Penguin's Dive

A torpedo in the sapphire water
Staring into the depths of the deep blue sea
With bubbles rushing past, the Emperor penguin swims.

From the penguin's magnificent view,
The silver bubbles darting past
Are like arrows that slice through the ocean.
The penguin's speed is so fast that a leopard seal
Cannot catch the torpedo.

**Lloyd Wallace (9)**
Port Regis School

## An Acorn

I go outside and hear a crunch,
A broken acorn on the ground,
A seed of life
That came from up above me in the canopy,
A canopy of leaves and branches.
I can only just see the sky,
A speck of blue,
But it is blue beyond the green.

**Christopher Brinkworth (11)**
**Port Regis School**

## Buster

Sitting obediently on the wooden floor,
Staring at a cat with his glaring eyes waiting to attack,
His wagging tail frozen by the flash of the camera,
Wondering what he would do if he caught the cat.
His black coat gleaming like polished shoes,
He breathes deeply,
Waiting for the cat to drop its guard,
So he can get a head start.

**Jack Robinson (10)**
**Port Regis School**

## What You Would Find In My Brother's Pocket

A dried up lollipop all covered in hair,
A month old tissue as solid as a rock,
A handful of sister's hair all over the lolly,
A plastic toy soldier with one arm missing,
A stick of gum all covered in crumbs,
Dried up glue all over the soldier's arm,
A plastic toy car with one wheel lost,
A Yu-gi-oh card all bent and creased.

**Freddie Ashford-Russell (10)**
**Port Regis School**

## She's Gone For Ever

I used to have a puppy called Chaos,
She wagged her tail as she walked.
Her face was so sweet.
When we went in the car,
We would put her in the boot
And she would jump over
Into the middle of the car.
She was a star at jumping
And when the car turned a corner,
She would lean to one side
And make a funny little face.

My puppy was as soft as velvet
And shone in the sun like crystal.
The colour of her shiny fur
Was golden yellow,
Like sweet honey in a pot.
Her soft, floppy, silky ears were so beautiful
And flopped over her sparkly eyes.
She had a black, wet, slippery nose
That gleamed in the sun.

I used to have a puppy called Chaos
Till one day she walked into the pool
And never came out again.

**Matilda Wilkinson (10)**
**Port Regis School**


## Golden Dates

The red, golden and orange colours
Of a carpet of dates,
High above the sundried fruit
Stand shaded trees.

The nearby road deserted,
The stained donkey resting under the trees.
All is silent in this land of colour.

**Connie Robins (9)**
**Port Regis School**

## Celebrate Your World

I celebrate the look of very long grass
Swaying in the wind
Like a candle flame, blown gently.

I celebrate the sound of my cat
Purring in all different tunes.

I celebrate the feel of the wind
Blowing in my face
On a windy day.

I celebrate the taste of chocolate
Melting on my tongue.

I celebrate the smell of bread
That has just been baked in a bakery.

I celebrate the memories
Of a holiday with my friends and family.

**Lucy Allison (10)**
Port Regis School


## Homer Simpson's Pocket

A few spare dollars from 1986,
A 6 pack of Duff beer cans (empty),
An address book,
A book about why he is alive which he does not use,
A pencil and pen,
A driving licence with someone else's photo on it,
A piece of half-eaten bubblegum,
A damaged pair of car keys,
Lisa's homework from 2 weeks ago,
And a present for Bart's fifth birthday.

**William von Behr (11)**
Port Regis School

## Disaster

My brother starts shouting across the beach,
I see a huge wall of water crashing down.

My family are already running.
Behind me,
The water towers over me -
Blackness!

Emerging from the water,
My head is spinning,
I wonder, where am I?
Am I still alive?
Looking around -
Devastation!
Families ripped apart.
Is mine?
Will I ever see them again?

**Flora McFarlane (10)**
**Port Regis School**


## The Volcano

Up from the chamber,
Rises lava into the vent.
Red-hot lava, like fireworks,
Lights up the sky.
The volcano sounds like a thousand guns firing in unison.
A fountain of fire,
Destroying hills, woods and trees . . .
The blazing inferno of doom.

**Ben Willbourn (9)**
**Port Regis School**

## The Day I Lost My Shoes

I couldn't find my shoes
So, seeing my mum's and dad's wellies,
I climbed into them.
My feet felt like the only pea in a big pod.
My mum witnessed me putting them on!

Clumping along, I made for the climbing frame.
I stumbled up the ladder
And slid down the slide.

Some ripe raspberries
Glowed in the sun
With a rumbling tummy, I waddled over.

Suddenly I saw a flash,
Mum had 'caught' me in the act!

**Emily Matthews (10)**
Port Regis School


## The Winter Acorn Tree

The cold, smooth texture of the acorn.
I can hear the sound of swaying branches,
The sound makes you feel sad and miserable.
The droplets of water loudly splash onto the leaves
And run off the leaf like a cat chasing a rabbit.
The million shades of green slowly tempt you
To stare as if you were paralysed.
As the end of the day comes the acorns drop off . . .
One by one.

**Hanifah Debono (11)**
Port Regis School

## Celebrate Your World

I celebrate the sound
Of popcorn popping in the microwave.
I celebrate the feel
Of my dog Buster's fur
All rough and spiky.
I celebrate the taste
Of chocolate, sinking into my tongue.
I celebrate the sight
Of my pony grazing in the field,
With the sun flickering and sparkling on her coat at sunset.
I celebrate the smell
Of chocolate cake just out of the oven.
I celebrate the memory
Of having fun with my friends.

**Scarlett Aichroth (9)**
**Port Regis School**


## In The Pocket Of A Soldier

Nine things in the pocket of a soldier . . .

The new improved handgun,
Silencer,
A magazine,
Bullets from World War II.

Maps of near areas,
Compass,
A knife that's all rusty,
Picture of his family,
He has got a beret to show his regiment.

**Henry Turpie (10)**
**Port Regis School**

## Snow Scene

Glittering crystals,
Shining white snow,
And the shadows of gloomy trees.
Snowflakes are thick
And sparkling in the air.
It looks as if the whole world
Has lit up
With the glittery, sparkling thick snow.
And the houses down in the village
Are white in the snow.
The rocky mountains
Are hilly and light.
The sharp, white silver crystals
Are sparkling in the sun.

**Thomas Mitchell (10)**
**Port Regis School**


## What's In Hermione Granger's Pocket

Hogwarts robes,
A pot of fizzy, magical potion,
A box of every star in the sky,
A wand,
A book of spells the size of a whale,
Everlasting jelly beans of all different flavours,
A broom, super fast Nimbus 2005,
Hermione's cat, Crookshanks,
A paper of her exam results - 100%!
A golden Snitch.

**Harriet Hedges (11)**
**Port Regis School**

## The Mummy

I am three thousand years old but I was fifty when I died.
I was a great ruler but not now.
I had a beautiful palace, but not now.
I look out of the eye holes of this tiny coffin
And how time goes on!
I see strange people coming into a room
Just to stare at me.
I see strange buildings being built
But I see my palace in a picture.
I am in a strange place
But I will always be the same.

**Jamie Horton (9)**
Port Regis School

## Snow

Trees silently dropping their leaves,
While footprints dent the milky snow.
Distant clouds watching over
As cars pass by.

Blue skies shining down,
With shadows of trees,
On the glistening snow.

Birds fluttering over the trees
With robins singing cheerfully.
Only one small tree
Pokes its crown over the frozen grass.

**Kathryn Francis (10)**
Port Regis School

## Winter In The Cristo Mountains

The soft snow
Like cotton wool
Covers the trees like a fluffy duvet.
Snowy stalactites hang from the fir branches
Glinting in the glowing sunlight.

Footprints dent the snow,
Through the shadows in the maze of trees
Watched over by the snow-topped mountains
And lonely wisps of cloud.

Villages of grasses
Huddle in the protection of the trees,
Waiting for the spring
So they can attack the snow.

The air feels fresh and crisp,
As a biting breeze drifts
The snowflakes float and settle
On the magical snow.

**Elizabeth Killick (9)**
Port Regis School


## Bishop

Placed on a chess board,
Protecting a king,
The bishop stares beadily forwards.
With his crook in his hand,
And his mitre on his head,
Waiting for the chance to come,
For him to take the knight on horseback
And move out of danger.
But the white bishop is scared that
The black will attack so he moves forward,
Trembling that he might die.

**Anders Horwood (9)**
Port Regis School

## Hong Kong Harbour

Tall buildings reaching into the sky,
Dwarfing the boats in the harbour.
Some modern flats cling to the mountainside
On which dense green trees live.

As the birds glide in the light blue sky,
People crowd in the ferry
Sailing across the blue-green water
About to go into the dirty harbour.

People shoving round the cheap market,
Shopkeepers huffing and puffing in the heat.
The lucky people have a snack,
Maybe some duck soup or some slippery noodles.

**Patrick Milne (10)**
Port Regis School

## The Jolly Roger II

Its bulky sails with the white cross that hangs on the mast,
With a hull of timber that's painted blue and brown.
They swing off a rope to board other ships
But when they miss,
They fall into the indigo-blue waters.
Ships nearby would see the sails and say, 'Pirates!'
If the sailors did not recognise the sails
It would be too late by the time they had seen the flag,
They would have been locked in heavy battle
For the flag is the skull and cross bones.
This ship is . . .
The Jolly Roger II.

**Tim Dickins (10)**
Port Regis School

## The Beach

Dark, gloomy shadows
Stretch along the level beach.

Beams of light shimmer across the breaking waves,
Slicing into the sand,
Racing against the inky clouds.

Murky cliffs surround the bay,
Rocks poised to fall on the smooth beach.

And through the raven clouds
A glimmer of hope,
A sparkle of light.

**Edward MacDonald (9)**
**Port Regis School**


## Dawn

Golden, amber light
Glows against the dark landscape.
Radiant orange ripples contrast the burnt umber heavens.
As the night expires
The dawn washes over it.
The sky mimics the sea with thundering waves
And rotating whirlpools.
The surface of the lake ruffles
As it reflects the black silhouettes of the evergreens.
The uninhabited wilderness is swept with warmth.
This fleeting moment is captured on film.

**Robin Brinkworth (9)**
**Port Regis School**

## Out For A Walk

Running faster and faster through the estuary;
The wind is pushing against my face,
Nellie and Coco run along in front,
I can't catch up.

Faster they run through the stream,
Both sprinting now.
They think life's a dream.

Nearly there now,
Almost home,
Panting, muddy, frothing
But satisfied.

**Jack Gething (9)**
**Port Regis School**


## Celebrate Your World

I celebrate the sight of butterflies
Fluttering in the summer breeze.

I celebrate the sound of bees buzzing
Sucking pollen from the flowers.

I celebrate the feel of warm, gooey mud
In my hands.

I celebrate the taste of candyfloss
Disappearing in my mouth.

I celebrate the happiness
Of making friends.

**Natasha O'Keeffe (9)**
**Port Regis School**

## Celebrate Your World

I celebrate the sound of the wind
Brushing against the trees
Like a feather duster.

I celebrate the sight of the warm fire's flames
Which change colour
And then disappear.

I celebrate the fresh, rich taste
Of mountainside water.

I celebrate the sweet smell of spring
When it comes into blossom.

I celebrate the feel of water
Flowing over my hands.

**William Roberts (9)**
**Port Regis School**


## Celebrate Your World

I celebrate the look of the tiger
The black and gold against the sun.
I celebrate the sound of the lion's roar
That makes me feel strong and mighty.
I celebrate the feel of my old dog's coat
Short and smooth.
I celebrate the taste of mango
Tangy and sweet.
I celebrate the memory of riding my chestnut mare
Back to her stable,
Nice and fast after a long ride.

**Oscar Appleby (10)**
**Port Regis School**

## The Lion

The hungry lion,
stalks its prey
through the long grass;
amber eyes watching,
waiting,
great mane shaking,
muscles flexing.
Moving in for the kill,
closer, closer,
mouth agape.
Breaks cover,
paws pounding,
claws dig in,
bringing it down -
the kill.

**Paul Collins (9)**
**Port Regis School**


## The Scarecrow

All alone in a pale yellow field,
His shoulders covered in bird droppings,
Stands the scarecrow.
A sorrowful smile, but full of love,
His dried out carrot nose all eaten away,
On his sad, unloved face.
The cold wind rushing through his coat,
With the broken buttons hanging and drooping.
Raggy trousers all patched and slashed.
But really, he is a useful fellow!

**Anna Gray (9)**
**Port Regis School**

## The Swan

Gliding through the water
With its long neck swaying from side to side
Came a beautiful swan.
Its graceful neck curved,
Its feet paddling fluently.

Ducking its head down underneath the shimmering water,
I hear sounds of splashing
As it searches for food -
And a low musical song.

Later, water dripping from its beak,
It raises its head;
Bright eyes glistening in the sun.

**Milly Hedges (9)**
Port Regis School

## The Starfish

The tide comes in
Washing a starfish
Into a rocky pool,
Leaving it stranded
With many other creatures.

Racing down the beach,
An orange glow in shallow water
Catches my eye.

On rocks and sand,
Five patterned legs
Lie cast ashore by the tide.

**Morgan Cronin-Webb (10)**
Port Regis School

## The Lost Memories

'Where has it all gone?'
'What?'
'Well everything!'
'What do you mean everything?'
'Well like . . .

That plastic dummy I sucked when I was one.'
'Oh I threw it away, it was revolting!'

'Well when I was two I had that plastic lion I chewed?'
'Chewed to pieces!'

'Oh, what about that music box that sang when I was three?'
'It ran out of song.'

'When I was four Dad bought me a red tricycle.'
'I gave it to your cousins, you were too big for it anyway.'

'Where's the book of animal poems you read me when I was five?'
'Your granny gave it to a charity shop, she said you'd read it all!'

'But those were my memories.'
'Yes, but you'll never use them again!'
'Well no, but they're still special.
So everything's gone?'
'Yes I suppose.'
'All of it? Everything! The whole lot?'
'Yes it's all gone . . .'

**Holly Isard (11)**
**Port Regis School**

## The Deer

Prancing in the sunlight,
Before the sun goes down.
Finding food for its helpless fawn,
Looking out for danger.

There're sounds of hunters' footsteps,
Creeping in the woodland area.
There's the noise of gunshots,
Only metres away.

Browsing on the leaves
Underneath thickets at dusk.
The snow is on the ground
And winter's coming.

**Eleanor Thwaites (9)**
Port Regis School


## Tiny Tim And The Trouble Twins

Tiny Tim and the trouble twins
In a tank killing their team
Tiny Tim sat on a tin
Tiny Tim and the trouble twins
Tiny Tim that is that
Tiny Tim and the trouble twins trapped the tiger's tail
Tiny Tim, tell that Tom
Tiny Tim and the trouble twins
Tackle that toad
Tiny Tim and the trouble twins
Tackle that ten
Tiny Tim tape that twig
Tiny Tim and the trouble twins
Trap that toad
Tiny Tim and the trouble twins
Take that tank
Tiny Tim and the trouble twins.

**Connor Pemberton (10)**
St Michael's Primary School, Lyme Regis

## Alphabet

A is for alliteration
B is for ballad
C is for clause
D is for dialogue
E is for elegy
F is for fable
G is for grapheme
H is for half rhyme
I is for inflection
J is for jargon
K is for kenning
L is for literacy
M is for myth
N is for narrative
O is for object
P is for poem
Q is for question
R is for rap
S is for skim
T is for tanka
U is for usage
V is for verb
W is for writing frame
X is for xenoglossia
Y is for yarn
Z is for zeugma.

**Bethany Allen (10)**
St Michael's Primary School, Lyme Regis

## Santa

Small, slimy Santa slipped slowly and silently onto the saddle
Sighing and singing then sighing said slowly, 'Shhhhhh.'
Sitting still, suddenly fell into sweet, silent, soft slumber
So soon Santa stood up suddenly and shouted, 'It is summer!'

**Henry Wadsworth (9)**
St Michael's Primary School, Lyme Regis

## Peter's Adventure

People pretending to be plumbers play poker,
Peter plays on the pitch,
While Paddy plays polo down a ditch,
Panthers pounce picking plants and puddles,
While piggies play getting in pickles,
The parrot paints pictures of the pond,
Pigs plant poppies and play ping-pong,
Peter the pod likes to party, party, party,
While pretending to panic and produce puzzles.

**Jessie Parker (10)**
St Michael's Primary School, Lyme Regis


## Little Lamar's Life

Little Lamar looks at a lake,
Little Lamar makes himself late.
Lazy Lucy looks at Little Lamar like she's not living,
Little Lamar looks at Lazy Lucy and starts larking.
Lazy Lucy starts shouting, 'Little Lamar stop before you
lose your lemonade,'
Little Lamar went to look at a lamb and fell, there he lay.

**Liam Trice (9)**
St Michael's Primary School, Lyme Regis


## Bad Bethany And Bossy Bill

Bad Bethany busted her bottom by banging bells,
But before Bethany bounced, Bill broke her belt.
So Brady broke Bill's big balloon
And Bill bellowed before belching, 'Beware Brady before
bursting black balloons.'
Bad Bethany bellowed, 'Bill, Brady bake baked beans and break it up.'
Bill and Brady baked their beans and began to *burp!*

**Sarah Nicholson (9)**
St Michael's Primary School, Lyme Regis

## Benny Bicwell

Benny began to bounce before bed,
Benny broke biscuits, bananas and bread.
Before Billy blinked in the bath
He changed his mind and switched to brass.
Moments later, Bethany's big belly belched by Bridport bakery.
Beware of Benny's bride, there are many things they want to hide.
Benny and Buster bent Billy's back,
Benny and Buster chucked him in the sack.

**Brady Wright (9)**
St Michael's Primary School, Lyme Regis


## Conor's Cat

Conor can catch Coca-Cola with Conor's cat
which can catch lots of bats.
Then Conor's cat got caught
and Conor's cat went to court.
They made Conor's cat go to a port
and made Conor's cat wear some shorts.
Then Conor's cat called for Conor
and Conor's cat and Conor escaped and celebrated with Donna.

**Zachary Rees-Haughton (9)**
St Michael's Primary School, Lyme Regis


## Jack And Jake

January, June, July, Jack and Jake are bored,
Jack and Jake go to the jungle
Jack got the job, 'Let's play, Jake,'
Jake saw Jack throw some animals jumping,
Just the dolls and Jake said,
'What's the jumping junk?'
Jack stood up and joked Jake and said,
'It's me Jack, ha, ha, ha!'

**Jack Chan (9)**
St Michael's Primary School, Lyme Regis

## Poodles

Poodles plant pumpkins in a pot,
Poodles drink pop,
Party pictures on a pig,
My papa is a pilot on a plane,
Peter had a patch to plant pumpkins,
Peter had a patch to plant pears,
People and punks get the pan while playing on a plane,
People carry pins in their pants so they can prick and pick themselves,
Poodles playing poker with pooches,
Pooches in Paris making pasta,
Pooches and poodles bite the postman,
Peter the poker goes and pokes the pooches,
Poodles chew on the post in the postbox,
Pigs playing in the pigsty,
Poodles in Paris and pooches, see pigs fly.

**Lorrayne White (10)**
St Michael's Primary School, Lyme Regis


## Someone Saw

Someone saw some sloths
Someone saw some spiders
Someone saw some sheep
Someone saw some shrimps in the sea
Someone saw some shipworms
Someone saw some shinnies
Someone saw some salamanders
Someone saw some sailfish
Someone saw some sand dollars
Someone saw some sea horses
Someone saw some saiga
Someone saw some sources.

**Oscar Gordon-Christopher (10)**
St Michael's Primary School, Lyme Regis

## ABC

A nnoying Andrew annoyed awful Alice
B ig Bob bounced in a blue balloon
C harlie the crocodile cracked a cornet
D oris the dinner lady danced on dumplings
E llie the elephant eats eggs every day
F at Fred fights ferociously
G race the goat greets gentlemen
H appy Harry helps in hospitals
I van the icicle ingests ink
J ake's job is a joking jester
K atie's king is Kyle
L orrayne loves licking lollies
M egan makes model Morris dancers
N aughty Nicole nicks nice notes
O liver opens opaque oranges
P erfect Peter pinches perfect ideas
Q ueen quivers quietly
R achael races rams
S ailor said, 'Salt the salmon.'
T revor taps turnips
U nsuccessful Ursula is uneven about umbrellas
V ain Violet is a ventriloquist
W alter waddles in water
X avier X-rays xylophones
Y asmin yells at yoghurt
Z ebras zoom out of zoos.

**Rachael Tipping (10)**
**St Michael's Primary School, Lyme Regis**

## Today And Tomorrow

Today I think
Tomorrow I take
I think, think and think
Today I thought
Tomorrow I taught
I taught, taught and taught.

**Archie Stoke Faiers (9)**
St Michael's Primary School, Lyme Regis


## Flying Fish

Fierce fire fiend Fred fries five flies for frogs from Forge forest floor.
Fake fat fish fly out of fishermen's boats and fill the flaky floor of the
fertile forest.
Next Fred the fire fiend's frightening cave fish fly from the cave
In forty formal fortresses to fashion factory for a fortune of fifteen
films and fax
But they fall from fever into the furious sea far below.

**Dominic Kirtley (10)**
St Michael's Primary School, Lyme Regis


## The Stormy Night Home

In the dark when lightning strikes
And rain pours like bullets from guns,
I tread on the slippery ground,
And when I step in puddles they splash.

I am nearly home, but still cold,
But I know when I am home,
It will bring to me my desired warmth,
And I will go and sit by the fire.

**Philipp Antonas (10)**
St Thomas Garnet's School, Bournemouth

## The Water Spirit

On the ocean's bottom, the glowing mosaic,
In the rotting shipwreck,
Lives the Water Spirit, glowing blue,
Her hair flowing behind,
Like a fire blowing this way and that,
Her hands are fading water.

She shall call to you, call your name,
Over and over, from the corners,
From the corners of her shipwreck.
Feel her breath,
Her icy breath, breathing upon your shoulder,
You turn and she's gone.

**Edward Parker (10)**
St Thomas Garnet's School, Bournemouth


## The Seasons

Spring is newborn lambs and butterflies too.
Summer is sun, water and fun.
Autumn is leaves rustling about.
Winter is snow, gleaming white.

Winter's gifts,
Autumn's love,
Summer's heat,
Spring's new life.

Spring is green and fresh,
Summer is yellow and lazy,
Autumn is russet and crisp,
Winter is white and magical.

**Bryony Cook (11)**
St Thomas Garnet's School, Bournemouth

## Number Four And Me!

For many years I was number three,
The little one was me,
But then along came number four,
A little boy who I adore.
He can't walk,
He can't talk,
He can't even play,
But my baby brother makes me happy each day.
I love his face,
I love his hands,
I love his feet
And more,
Even through he screams and shouts,
He's still my lovely number four.
His big blue eyes,
His rosy cheeks,
His sunny little smile,
His chubby legs,
His tiny toes,
He makes everything worthwhile.
If only numbers one and two
Could make me feel this way,
I would be so happy, every minute of the day!

**Amber Porter (8)**
**St Thomas Garnet's School, Bournemouth**


## When Clouds Will Rain

When clouds will rain and shadows will fall,
And thunder will roar,
And then it will pour.
And the flashing light will flash.
And the flashing light will flash.
Alone in the dark he sits,
A small boy scared to bits.

**William Porter (11)**
**St Thomas Garnet's School, Bournemouth**

## The Haunted House

The large old house stood still on the hill
where once there had stood an old working mill.
The trees hung over and shadowed the door,
you could hardly see the knocker anymore.

Inside, the cobwebs loomed large with spiders,
they looked rather like great, black gliders.
The smell was like damp, rotten and mould,
you could see your breath, it was so very cold.

People spoke of seeing witches and ghosts
looking out of windows and swinging from bedposts.
The floorboards on the stairs cracked and creaked,
you had to be careful you didn't hurt your feet.

I never will venture to that old house again,
where I think people once must have suffered much pain.
Hopefully one day the tortured spirits will rest
and the house once again will look its best.

**Daniel Doherty (10)**
**St Thomas Garnet's School, Bournemouth**


## When Land Meets Sea

When land meets sea
And waves crash upon the shore,
The waves that have travelled long miles
From places near and far,
Up and down, up and down,
Hitting the waiting land calmly.

When land meets sea
And hits stones, pebbles and jagged rocks,
The waves like creases in a shirt
Ironed out as they lap the shore,
Lapping the shore quietly or loudly,
Hitting the waiting land calmly.

**Robert Degan (11)**
**St Thomas Garnet's School, Bournemouth**

## Friends

Friends are generous,
Friends are kind,
The best of friends
Are hard to find.

So when you've found one,
Treat them with care,
Because a true friend
Will always be there.

In good times and bad,
When you're happy or sad,
A best friend will be with you,
Which makes you very glad.

I have a best friend called Harriett,
We've been friends since we were two,
We have fun doing things together,
Even when we're sitting on the loo!

**Hannah Doyle (9)**
**St Thomas Garnet's School, Bournemouth**

## Colours

When angry I think of black,
Then yellow holds me back.
Red is soothing, so is white,
Orange is a kite.
Pink is for girls, so is purple,
Green is a leaf moving about.
Blue is when you go and shout.
Mauve is for when you sleep,
Grey is for the people you meet.
Brown is for me,
The colour of dark, creamy chocolate too,
In my colourful dreams.

**Rebecca Lucy Murphy (10)**
**St Thomas Garnet's School, Bournemouth**

## The Very Clever Dog

There is a very clever dog,
His coat is as white as snow,
He has eyes extra blue,
I'm glad he will not go.

'My favourite food is
Biscuits, jam, peas and rice,
Bread and cheese,
But I don't like mice.

I like to ride my bike,
I always chew my bone,
I play on the computer,
And I ring on the phone.

I like it here in this house,
I am never sad,
I will never, ever go,
I'm very, very glad.'

**Matthew Giddens (7)**
St Thomas Garnet's School, Bournemouth

## Skating

My passion is to skate,
Don't lodge a complaint.
I always try to skate,
Me and my mates,
I don't know the date
Because when I skate,
It makes me late.
I nearly missed the school fête
Because I love to skate,
Especially with my mates.

**Lewis Hawkins (8)**
St Thomas Garnet's School, Bournemouth

## Questions?

Questions asked, but never an answer.
Will I ever be a dancer?
How do fish stay under the sea?
If they can, why can't we?

Where does the sun go when we're asleep?
Does it collapse into a great big heap?
Is the sea green or blue?
We should ask an old boat's crew!

They say snowflakes are never alike,
Did they travel the world on a snowy hike?
Why are windows made of glass?
When you meet a glazier, why not ask?

Why doesn't money grow on trees?
Why are there stripes on bumblebees?
Why are babies small and adults big?
Why do judges all wear wigs?

Who made the words that we all use
To ask questions and tell the news?
Who made God? I haven't a clue!
But when I see Him, I'll ask Him for you!

**Amber Cook (9)**
**St Thomas Garnet's School, Bournemouth**


## Summer

Summer, summer, what a wonderful thing,
Down the beach having a swim.
Summer, summer, how nice it feels
To be in the sun, and in the fields.
Summer, summer, how fun it is,
To skip and run all day in the sun.
Summer, summer, what can I say?
Summer's such a great thing, *yay!*

**Allie Kenward (10)**
**St Thomas Garnet's School, Bournemouth**

## Seasons

I love it in springtime
When the birds begin to sing.
I love it in the summer
When I hear the church bells ring.

I love it in the autumn
When the leaves begin to fall.
Most of all I love it in the winter
As a certain person starts to call.

**Jasmine Elliot (10)**
St Thomas Garnet's School, Bournemouth

## My Friends

My friends at school
Are kind and cool,
I play with them every day,
Unless they're ill or on holiday.

They come to my house, I go to theirs,
We go to the cinema, we go to fairs.
The thing we like most when we're sitting on our seats
Is to eat loads and loads and loads of *sweets*.

**Katie Spencer (9)**
St Thomas Garnet's School, Bournemouth

## My Pets

At home I have three dogs,
They all love sitting on logs.
When we take them for a walk,
They sit and listen to us talk.

My oldest is called Paddy,
My second oldest is called Poppy,
My youngest is called Mac
And sometimes he gets a big smack.

**Jessica Smith (10)**
St Thomas Garnet's School, Bournemouth

## Snowy

Hi!
My name is Snowy,
I'm not very old.
I live in the snow,
But I don't like the cold.
I sleep alone on an icy bed
And I dream that I'm cosy
And cuddled instead.
You look like someone
Who's kind,
Can I come to your house?
Don't leave me behind.
Then when the night
Is all chilly,
Cuddle me close
And be warm with your *Snowy!*

**Harriett Wragg (9)**
**St Thomas Garnet's School, Bournemouth**


## The Great Horse

Jogging along, trotting along,
Through the wood,
Twisting and turning,
Lovely soft fur,
Lovely soft tail.

Dark wood, very dark,
Horse is asleep,
Fast asleep.

I eat lovely hay and straw,
I am a very sad horse.

**Kate Glanville (7)**
**St Thomas Garnet's School, Bournemouth**

## The Very Smart Eagle

I am an eagle.
I have beautiful grey skin
And a yellow, sharp beak.
I have black pointy feet
And I also have blue, cunning eyes.

This is what I do.
I soar through the air
And I swoop down to catch my prey.

This is what I have for my prey.
I have mice
And rabbit.

I am very fierce.

**Jean-Jacques Coppini (8)**
St Thomas Garnet's School, Bournemouth


## James

My baby brother James
Was born in July.
He's always happy
And never cries.

Every night he has a bath,
He's always splashing
And we all laugh.

I can't wait until he grows up
And goes to school,
And then he can join in all our games,
Including football.

**Jack Palmer (10)**
St Thomas Garnet's School, Bournemouth

## I Have To Write A Poem

I have to write a poem,
It has to be done tonight.
I'm not very good,
I highly doubt that I'm going to get this right.

I don't know what to write!
What I need is an idea.
I could call a friend,
I know, I'll call Mia.

I called her,
She doesn't have a clue,
I'm really stuck,
What am I going to do?

I might as well give up,
It'll be midnight before I'm done,
But my teacher will have a fit,
This is really not fun.

I don't see the point
In writing this down,
The more I think,
The more I frown.

This is making me feel sick,
My head's starting to spin,
I might as well
Throw this in the bin.

This is doing my head in,
I just don't get it.
I want to watch EastEnders,
But I haven't even done the first bit!

Wait a minute, I can watch EastEnders!
I've just written a poem!

**Landi Wagner (10)**
**St Thomas Garnet's School, Bournemouth**

## Slow Snail

Why are snails so slow, I wonder?
Slithering down the path.
I nearly trod on one last week,
But dodged and fell on the grass.
Everybody hates them,
I don't know why,
But I dodge every time, I do,
And everybody laughs!

**Jessica Balfour (7)**
St Thomas Garnet's School, Bournemouth


## The Peacock

I like the peacock,
It looks like this,
It has many coloured feathers,
Black, orange and blue.
I think it has a feeling to be happy.
The peacock makes me happy too.

**Taylor Rees (8)**
St Thomas Garnet's School, Bournemouth


## Cheetah

What does it look like?
The cheetah looks scary
With white, shining teeth.
What does it do?
It runs very, very fast.
What is its prey?
It hunts zebras and deer.

**Diarmid Becker (8)**
St Thomas Garnet's School, Bournemouth

# Poems

Poems can be about anything.
Some are a bit hazy,
Some are definitely crazy.
Some can be completely mad,
Some can be very sad.
What do you prefer?
Speak out, don't mutter.

Poems can be about anything.
Some are about people being yappy,
Some are about people being happy.
Some are weak and feeble,
Some are just about people.
What do you prefer?
Speak out, don't mutter.

Poems can be about anything.
Some are amazingly funny,
Some are about sticky honey.
Some describe slimy lizards,
Some describe magic wizards.
What do you prefer?
Speak out, don't mutter.

Poems can be about anything.
Some make you feel glad,
Some are just completely bad.
Some are childish and silly,
But none are about my cat Billy.
What do you prefer?
Speak out, don't mutter.

**Nadia Foy (8)**
**St Thomas Garnet's School, Bournemouth**

## A Fish . . . To Be Or Not To Be?

If I could make a wish,
I'd like to be a fish.

I'd swim away across the bay
To an island not so far away.

To laugh and play all day
In the summer wonderland
Of sea and sand.

Cruising the ocean
Where dolphins roam in motion,
To a new destination.

Seagulls fly high in the sky,
Swirling and twirling, floating on clouds
And squawking out loud.

On my return to harbour,
Boats blow to starboard,

So I follow the markers
To calmer waters.

But what if I get caught?
A dreadful thought.
Barbecued, roasted or toasted,
A fish on someone's dish.

On second thoughts,
I'd much rather be a . . . ?

**Christie Quinn (8)**
**St Thomas Garnet's School, Bournemouth**

## The New Puppy

I have a brand new puppy,
She is so cute and fluffy.
Her name is Honey,
She is very funny.
She chews her toys,
And makes lots of noise.
She nibbles my toes,
And kisses my nose.
I love her such a lot,
She is the bestest friend that I've got.

**Amy Mack Nava (8)**
St Thomas Garnet's School, Bournemouth

## Coral, Coral

Coral, coral on the sea floor,
I wish you could grow
So much more.
You clean the sea
And make it look pretty.
You offer safe haven
For small, tiny fishes.

**Charles Tizzard (8)**
St Thomas Garnet's School, Bournemouth

## Leopard

L eopard leaping long strides.
E ating meat he kills.
O strich is his meal.
P rancing with pride.
A round him it is hot and sunny.
R unning with speed and beauty.
D angerous is the dancing leopard.

**Henry Newton (9)**
St Thomas Garnet's School, Bournemouth

## My Cat

My cat is very clever,
She goes out in any weather,
She catches all the frogs and mice,
Even on the ice.

My cat is very clever,
She climbs all the trees
And chases all she sees.

During the day she sleeps,
Saving all her energy to leap.
She tiptoes on the fence,
Nobody knows the secrets which she keeps.

My cat is always washing,
She keeps her paws and tail clean.
You would never know where she had been.
My cat's garden is my nanny's dream,
She always gives my cat cream.
Sometimes in the garden you may see a bat,
Or is it that darn cat!

My cat explores all around,
She hardly makes a sound.
She's as dainty as a feather,
And her paws are as soft as leather.

My cat likes to sit by the pond,
She's as cunning as James Bond.
She likes to watch the fish,
And she would have them as her dish.

My cat never scratches
And she can open all the latches.
She takes herself to bed,
And that's enough said.

**Alexander Drake (8)**
**St Thomas Garnet's School, Bournemouth**

## Pet Shops

One day I went into a pet shop and saw:

First a snake that was
Slippery and long,
Slithering, slithering.

Next a hamster that was
Cute, small and cuddly,
Squeaking, squeaking.

Then a kitten that was
Tiny and small,
Purring, purring.

Last a puppy that was
Lively and happy,
Barking, barking.

**Catherine Shelton (9)**
St Thomas Garnet's School, Bournemouth

## Colours

Blue, brown, orange, green,
So many colours to be seen.
The grass is green,
The sky is blue,
The sun is yellow
When shining through.
White clouds,
Grey ones too,
I love colours,
Do you?

**Maria Degan (9)**
St Thomas Garnet's School, Bournemouth

## My Sister, Amelia Katerina

A is for angel, *not,* Amelia is a pain.
M is for *mega trouble* when she shoots down the lane.
E is for excited at the slightest little thing.
L is for love, she makes my heart sing.
I is for irritating when she messes with my stuff.
A is for Amelia, I just can't love her enough.

K is for kind, when she holds my hand.
A is for angry, when she just can't understand.
T is for tiny, little hands and feet.
E is for every little smile that looks so sweet.
R is for rank, when she does a smelly nappy.
I is for ice cream, that makes her happy.
N is for naughty, when she tries to be tough.
A is for Amelia, I just can't love her enough.

**Alexandra Hibberd (8)**
St Thomas Garnet's School, Bournemouth

## The Calm, Wavy Beach

With the waves you feel calm,
With the sun you feel warm.
The waves splash along the shore,
You can relax when the sun's full.

You can see the sailing boats going along,
See the view of the sea that carries on,
The sun starts to come down the beach, time is over,
We start to pack up to go back home.

**Ersan Beskardes (9)**
St Thomas Garnet's School, Bournemouth

## My Christmas Surprise

'What do you want for Christmas?' my parents said to me.
I said, 'I'd like a gerbil, a special friend to be.'
My parents said, 'No way.'
But on Christmas Day that year,
I opened up a pressie and didn't know what to say.

It was better than my camera, and better than my book,
A tiny little creature, who was giving me a look.
He lets me stroke him day or night,
And never does he bite.
Skittles is my gerbil's name, I think he's really tame.

He's fast and grey, he's got brown eyes,
He was my greatest Christmas surprise!

**Oliver Yeadon (8)**
St Thomas Garnet's School, Bournemouth


## Winter Vs Spring

Winter vs spring,
The fight will begin.
Warmth vs cold,
The story is told.

A kick in the back,
Great power he lacks,
A blow to the head,
He's surely dead.

Spring leaps high,
He cannot die.
Winter lays still,
Unable to kill.

Spring is now back,
Winter has slacked,
He falls with a bump,
And a great, loud flump!

**Joshua Green (11)**
Salway Ash CE VA Primary School

## As Wet As The Sea

As wet as the sea - as dry as the Sahara desert,
As hot as a devil - as cold as thick ice,
As lively as a dog - as dull as a snail,
As thin as a snake - as bulging as hippos,
As soft as a cat - as fierce as a tiger,
As light as a feather - as heavy as a truck,
As strong as a diamond - as weak as some paper,
As curly as hair - as straight as a plank,
As fine as a thread - as thick as some rope,
As long as a bus - as short as a key,
As wily as Einstein - as dumb as a dodo,
As brittle as glass - as tough as gristle,
As good as a feast - as bad as a witch,
As blunt as a hammer - as sharp as a pin,
As flat as a flounder - as round as a ball,
As choppy as the sea - as calm as a plain,
As proud as a peacock - as blithe as a grig,
As bold as a thief - as sly as a fox,
As slow as a tortoise - as fast as the wind,
As true as the gospel - as false as mankind,
As fierce as a tiger - as mild as a dove,
As tight as a drum - as free as the air,
As plain as a pike-staff - as rough as a bear,
As steady as time - uncertain as the weather,
As stiff as a poker - as limp as a glove.

**Matthew Pyett (10)**
**Salway Ash CE VA Primary School**


## Fear

Fear looks as sharp as the sharpest pin as it sinks into your skin.
Fear feels cold as the coldest ice and as wet as the sea.
Fear smells like a dead body rotting in its grave.
Fear tastes like the most bitter of lemons.
Fear reminds me of a burning flame.

**Blaine Davis (10)**
**Salway Ash CE VA Primary School**

## Weather Wars

I'm an invisible assassin.
I stab you in the back
With my ice-cold dagger.
My ally is winter,
And my foe is summer.
I am a spirit that howls
And taps on your window.
What am I?
I am wind.

I warm your neck
And fight wind.
I am like MI6 floating in the sky,
Getting rid of all bad weather.
What am I?
I am sun.

**Jack Hill (10)**
**Salway Ash CE VA Primary School**


## The Devil

The Devil is always watching you
Committing all your crimes.
If you fall into his trap,
That is the end of your time.

The Devil will drag you back down to Hell,
When you're drifting off to Heaven.
No one knows his real name,
But they think he's called Satan.

Remember, remember,
The Devil's always watching,
Watching you and your family.
If you step out of line,
You'd better step back
Before you're out of time.

**George Sparks (10)**
**Salway Ash CE VA Primary School**

## My No 1 Mum
*(Inspired by 'The Dark Avenger')*

My mum is the kindest mum in the world.
'Get to your room, now!'

If I am feeling sad, she is great to talk to.
'Just get on with your homework!'

When I don't eat my vegetables she is very understanding.
'Fine then you won't get any.'

When I am not ready for school, she allows me time.
'Right then, I will go without you!'

If I ask for sweets she gives a brilliant excuse.
'I haven't got any change on me and they're bad for your teeth.'
(When really she has.)

I think that I have the best mum in the world,
Even if she shouts at me every so often!

**Laura Alexander (10)**
**Salway Ash CE VA Primary School**


## What Is It?

In the murky depths it dwells,
Wallowing in the mud.
It mutters to itself
And sings a little song,
Before finding beauty
And killing comes again,
Until it has its money.

The guilt has overcome it
And soon it is dead,
But dwell it does inside you
And then it comes again!

A: Hatred.

**Aidan Simson (10)**
**Salway Ash CE VA Primary School**

## Sisters!
*(In the style of Tony Bradman)*

'Can I wear your new top, Emma?'
'Um . . . let me think. *No!*'
'Ah, please!'
*'No!'*
'Please, please can I?'
'I said *no!*'
'I will tell Mum and Dad.'
'Go on. You won't though.'
'You want to bet? Mum! Dad!'
'All right, all right.'

'Do you know what?'
'What?'
'I didn't want to wear your new top anyway.'
'Yes you did.'
'No, I didn't.'
'Yes you did . . .'

**Jessica Kennedy (10)**
**Salway Ash CE VA Primary School**


## Stallion

Graceful, power,
The stallion, rearing, striking his legs,
Running wild, racing with the wind,
His coat glistening in the sun,
The sound of hoofbeats thumping on the ground,
Nostrils flaring,
His ears straight back as he smells the air,
Suddenly a chase . . .
The howl of the wolves is all that drones in the cold air
As the stallion gallops off into the vast horizon.

**Katrina Roberts (10)**
**Salway Ash CE VA Primary School**

## My Pet Snail

My pet snail
Has a friend who's a quail.
He's got a winning beat,
Called 'Without Any Feet'.

My pet snail
Is about to bolt,
I don't know why, I just got out the salt.
I trip and fall
Over my ball.

My pet snail
Starts to sizzle and burn.
Hey wait! I want a turn.
My pet is nearly dead, I cry,
He's hitting the bucket, about to die.

My pet cat
Is very fat,
His favourite food is fried fish
In his own cat fish-dish.

My pet cat
Is very fat,
His second favourite food is fried rat.
He's much better than my um . . .
Oh yeah, my pet snail who died, *sniff*.

**Holly Parkes (10)**
**Salway Ash CE VA Primary School**


## Traffic Lights

Red, stop,
Amber, stand by,
Green, foot down, off we go.
Traffic light red, amber, green, zoom,
Boom, crash!

**Marcus Crew (10)**
**Salway Ash CE VA Primary School**

## The Boy From Melplash

There was a young boy from Melplash,
Who liked to have a big, massive splash,
And also at school
He was very cool,
Because he was quick in a dash.

**Ben Hawkins (11)**
**Salway Ash CE VA Primary School**

## The War

Plans to start the war
To take over,
Bombs flying through the air,
Like rain coming from the sky,
Destroying our land.
We want peace,
They want war,
So we fight for our land,
We shall not give up.
Who has won?
We shall decide sooner or later,
But we won't give up.

**Callum Flawn (9)**
**Salway Ash CE VA Primary School**

## The Swirl

The swirl, it goes round and round,
Spinning, turning upside down,
Round and round, upside down,
Nowhere to turn, the swirl it swirls,
Turning backwards and forwards,
Side to side, it had better stop before it . . .

**Jordon Taylor (9)**
**Salway Ash CE VA Primary School**

## Old Man From Wales

There was an old man from Wales
Who loved to collect animals' tails,
He picked up his knife,
Nearly cut up his wife,
So stopped collecting animals' tails.

**Abigail Hoskins (9)**
**Salway Ash CE VA Primary School**


## The Key And The Rat

He was a cunning little fiend,
An eye as sharp as a knife.
He ran through the town
Showing off his new crown.

Within a second he was on a boat,
Down, down, down,
Until he was at his nest with his ten little cubs,
But only five will survive.

**Spike Duff (9)**
**Salway Ash CE VA Primary School**


## Pet Cat

I love my pet cat,
But it's too madly fat.
It loves to chase rats,
It's terrified of bats.
When I sat on the sofa . . .
*Miaooow!*
I sat on my cat.

**Jamal Hadj-Aissa (10)**
**Salway Ash CE VA Primary School**

## Darkness

Darkness reminds me of being alone.
Darkness feels like a dark monster.
Darkness looks like a black pitch.
Darkness sounds like shouting and fear.
Darkness tastes like cold air.
Darkness smells like something unpleasant.

**Amy Bodycombe (10)**
**Salway Ash CE VA Primary School**


## Summer - Cinquain

It's hot,
The sea is cold.
The sea has lots of people.
Run in, cool off, it's very nice.
I'm cool.

**Alicia Chambers-Hill (10)**
**Salway Ash CE VA Primary School**


## Love

Love tastes like luscious, ripe, red strawberries
and rich, yellow cream.
Love smells like a forest of bright, sweet-smelling flowers
fluttering in a soft, warm breeze.
Love sounds like relaxing, gentle, flowing music.
Love looks like an angel in a flowing silk dress
with thick golden hair to her waist.
Love reminds me of a solid gold, heart-tipped arrow.

**Mini Warren (11)**
**Salway Ash CE VA Primary School**

## What Am I?

I'm big and black and green.
I fly but my wings can't move,
And I have wheels.
What am I?

*A: An army plane.*

**Joshua Baker (10)**
**Salway Ash CE VA Primary School**


## Sadness

Sadness looks as cold as an iceberg.
It smells like blood burning, sadness and fear,
It looks like people red-eyed and ready to burst into tears.
It sounds like shouting people crying and all emotional.
It reminds me of a flame of fire.
It tastes like something you can't eat, bringing back bad memories.

**Joshua Sprague (10)**
**Salway Ash CE VA Primary School**


## Dinosaur Roar

The allosaurus snores,
But when he wakes up, he roars.
He always does the chores,
Like eating wild boars.
Then he runs back to the moors
And snores.

**Adam Rhodes (9)**
**Salway Ash CE VA Primary School**

## Bug Bath

There's a bug in the bath
And it's having a laugh.
It'll get out the bath
Then it'll walk up the path.

So it walked up the path
And had another laugh.
Then it wasn't very funny,
Cos it met a big fat bunny!

Then he went back home
And chewed on a comb.
Then it jumped on the light
And he had an awful fright . . .
Cos he fell in a bath
And had another . . . laugh.

**Naomi Davidson (10)**
**Salway Ash CE VA Primary School**


## On A Dark, Dark Night

On a dark, dark night
In a dark, dark graveyard,
A dark, dark figure,
An animal, a person?
Slinking past the gravestones
It stops, it crouches,
A harsh voice shouts, *'Cut!'*
The lights click on,
The poodle yaps and wags her tail.
'That's the end of scene two,'
The director says.
'Time for a break.'

**Gemma Smith (11)**
**Salway Ash CE VA Primary School**

## Fear

Fear is running away from a pack of wolves,
It smells like the spooky, dark, big wolves in the darkest,
spookiest forest ever.
Fear is opening the door of a big room,
It sounds like the frightening, haunted, gloomy, horrible room
With the darkest ever wardrobe.
Fear is a ghost behind my back when I don't know,
It feels like the disgusting, creepy, white, bad-looking ghost behind
my back.
Fear is curry sauce in my mouth,
It tastes like the booming hot, spicy curry sauce from a curry
in a frying pan.
Fear is a cave frightened by people,
It looks like the dark, spooky, dreadful cave down the windy road.

**Carla Jordan (8)**
**Sandford St Martin's CE VA First School**


## Love

Love is like the sweet-scented flowers,
It smells like the first day of the twinkling spring.
Love is like the fast beats of a pure gold heart,
It sounds like a big rabbit, feet jumping on the hard ground.
Love is like powerful magic in the sparkling air,
It feels like soft clouds in my hand.
Love is like pink, dreamy marshmallows,
It tastes like strawberry clouds in my mouth.
Love is like fluffy confetti in the air,
It looks like feathers falling to the ground.

**Connie Woodworth (8)**
**Sandford St Martin's CE VA First School**

## Fear

It smells like fire coming from a big barbecue
That is as big as a whiteboard.
Fear is a massive danger sign,
It sounds like when you hear lightning
Speedily strikes a tall tree.
Fear is deep, deep water,
It feels like an earthquake that hits a huge house and it erupts.
Fear is big, burning matchsticks,
It tastes like blood when you badly cut your hand
And have a drink of juice.
Fear is when you are at the top of a thin, tall tower
That is as big as 30 houses put together.
It looks like small falling rocks,
That look like small falling people,
That are very, very small.

**Jacob Rolls (7)**
**Sandford St Martin's CE VA First School**


## Fear

Fear is an alien, creeping all around space.
It smells like aliens' stinky black socks on their feet.
Fear is an earthquake shaking so hard you would fall over 100 times,
It sounds like huge giants stomping all over town.
Fear is being so high that you would shiver like a jelly,
It feels like when you go to the edge, you will fall off.
Fear is sand blowing into your face, you can't see a thing,
It tastes like a sandstorm as sand crumbles in your mouth.
Fear is the deep sea, with big waves bouncing up and down,
It looks like a swimming pool so deep you could *drown*.

**Jennifer Auger (7)**
**Sandford St Martin's CE VA First School**

## Happiness

Happiness is like silly funny clowns dancing to the tap dance,
It smells like birthday cake waiting for you to nibble on it and
Making you feel joy and cheerful in your heart.
Happiness is like goats chasing you around the field
For food and chewing on your shoelaces,
It sounds like gentle, welcoming, bright, glorious, cheerful,
Jolly, friends singing and prancing.
Happiness is like a big smiley balloon waving in the air,
It feels like drops of boiling, sweating, blazing, red-hot sunshine,
Happiness is like a swarm of butterflies, flying, swooping,
Ducking around your head,
It tastes like yummy, melting, glowing, heating cherries,
That are golden yellow,
Happiness is like an enormous big, cuddly teddy in your arms,
It looks like singing, tweeting, swooping birds swirling in the apple tree.

**Amy Shepherd (8)**
**Sandford St Martin's CE VA First School**


## Fear

Fear is a ginormous T-rex bashing down trees,
It smells like a fire that's burning madly.
Fear is an earthquake,
It sounds like a china set breaking quickly.
Fear is a grimy, old, dusty haunted house,
It feels like there are cobwebs as soft as silk everywhere.
Fear is a fierce, great white shark,
It tastes like a sour plum, as sour as a still, fizzy drink.
Fear is a booming monster, as loud as a tank,
It looks like it's going to gobble me up.

**Remy White (7)**
**Sandford St Martin's CE VA First School**

# Fear

Fear is a roaring dinosaur,
It smells like damp on a spider's web.
Fear is yellow with black stripes,
It sounds like a crocodile egg shaking.
Fear is a lizard with green leaves,
It feels like an empty dinosaur's footprint.
Fear is being chased by a lion,
It tastes like snakes' blood.
Fear is a leopard that's creeping up behind you,
It looks like a zebra running.

**Charlie Jones  (7)**
Sandford St Martin's CE VA First School


# Shyness

Shyness is working in a new class,
It smells like a nasty new home.
Shyness is meeting people I don't know,
It sounds like fighting in the forest.

**Thomas Hawkins  (8)**
Sandford St Martin's CE VA First School


# Fear

Fear is guard dogs guarding all the gold,
It smells like the explosion of fire in the garden.
Fear is one big punch in the face, really hard,
It sounds like a terrifying giant walking along the world.
Fear is lightning going against a house window,
It feels like a crumbling rock, crumbling in my hand.
Fear is a giant wave coming towards the town,
It tastes like the strawberry Chewitts crunching in my mouth.
Fear is a whack in the face,
It looks like the boiling hot, shining sun!

**Ryan Adams  (7)**
Sandford St Martin's CE VA First School

## Happiness

Happiness is a hamster where he runs with delight,
It smells like his cage has been just cleaned.
Happiness is my friends laughing with joy,
It sounds like a hamster running in his wheel.
Happiness is a roast dinner, it looks tasty,
It tastes like ice cream, it gets warm in my hot mouth.
Happiness is vanilla ice cream, I love it,
It looks like my mum, as playful as a bumblebee.

**Dylan Crook (7)**
**Sandford St Martin's CE VA First School**


## Happiness

Happiness is a graceful ballerina,
Is smells like a gorgeous rose,
Happiness is a beautiful fairy,
It sounds like a spectacular singer,
Happiness is an elephant whooshing,
Their trunk in the magnificent sunset.

**Elli Masterton (7)**
**Sandford St Martin's CE VA First School**


## Happiness

Happiness is the blue sky, blowing a blue flag,
it smells like the sea when the salt comes, raw fish come by.
Happiness is making sandcastles, then knocking them down again,
And when I see my cousin.
It sounds like people talking about their favourite toy.
Happiness is playing when I play with my cousin,
It feels like the sea going up and down over the waves,
Jet skis whizzing along at 100 miles an hour.
Happiness is chocolate when it's crunchy.

**Harry Rose (7)**
**Sandford St Martin's CE VA First School**

## Loneliness

Loneliness is frogs that are as green as grass and leaves on trees,
It smells like smelly, sweaty socks.
Loneliness is blunt, long, thin pencils scratching on paper,
It sounds like rubbers deleting writing.
Loneliness is reading rough, sad books which make people cry,
It feels like hedgehogs snuffling in the night, they feel soft
                                                    on the tummy.
Loneliness is turkeys gobbling around in their pen,
It tastes like crisps crunching and crumbling in my mouth.
Loneliness is benches that feel all wooden, smooth and gappy,
It looks like trees that are as tall as a giant crushing the town.

**Amber Jackson (8)**
**Sandford St Martin's CE VA First School**


## Love

Love is an exciting present from my mum,
It smells like a sweet red rose blowing in the cool breeze.
Love is sticky, sour sweets,
It sounds like a flowing river.
Love is a big, huge surprise,
It feels like an enormous cuddle from my mum.
Love is a big smile from my best friend,
It tastes like a box of dark brown, orange cream chocolates.
Love is a kiss and cuddle, goodnight,
It looks like a dolphin splashing in the waves.

**Amber Baker (7)**
**Sandford St Martin's CE VA First School**

## Shyness

Shyness is like a spy searching for a robber
With the latest jewels,
It smells like a robber robbing their precious jewels,
Shyness is like a scurrying red spider running from clumsy feet,
It sounds like people whispering about you,
Shyness is like running mice scurrying from a big, bad cat,
It feels like you are the tiny, little girl and the world is the biggest place,
Shyness is like a butterfly fluttering from a scary jumping cat,
It tastes like the newest medicine slipping down my throat,
Shyness is like a spilling teardrop splashing from a
Little girl crying for her mum.
It looks like other children playing with their friends
And you are alone.

**Bethan Harcourt (8)**
**Sandford St Martin's CE VA First School**


## Fear

Fear is zombies chasing behind you,
It smells like zombies, smelly like a pair of rotten old socks.
Fear is exploding earthquakes,
It sounds like a solid rock bashing against the earth.
Fear is violent, snapping piranhas,
It feels like a piece of chocolate sprinkling in my hand.
Fear is pink marshmallows,
It tastes like a soft, squidgy thing melting in my mouth.
Fear is a spooky ghost going, 'Whooo!'
It looks like an empty, white sheet of paper.

**Oliver Meaden (7)**
**Sandford St Martin's CE VA First School**

## Fear

Fear is a huge, ground-shaking earthquake.
It smells like the quick, nasty, bloodthirsty wolves.
Fear is big, huge, sharp spikes,
It sounds like a big, spooky wardrobe.
Fear is a big, noisy thunderstorm,
It feels like the horrible, wet, sharp injection.
Fear is a massive white ghost,
It tastes like the huge African spider.
Fear is a violent great white shark,
It looks like the enormous, brain-eating zombies.

**James Blakesley (8)**
**Sandford St Martin's CE VA First School**


## Happiness

Happiness is my friend,
It smells like the burning bacon in the oven.
Happiness is the sweltering sun,
It sounds like PE booming in the hall.
Happiness is a fun holiday,
It feels like me and my friends are holding hands having fun.
Happiness is Christmas, opening up all the presents,
It tastes like my dog jumping up at me when he is wet.
Happiness is my pet dog jumping up at me when he is excited,
It looks like Christmas is coming, and the presents are being sent.

**Sarah Richards (7)**
**Sandford St Martin's CE VA First School**

# Fear

Fear is a slimy green monster as it tiptoes out of the closet,
It smells like the red, raw, runny blood of a whale shark's prey.
Fear is a cat falling from the tallest, crumbliest tower of the world,
It sounds like the big, loud roar of a T-rex dinosaur.
Fear is a dog being washed away in a tsunami,
It feels like waking up and the light shaped like a ghost.
Fear is a hammerhead shark hammering its prey,
It tastes like the potion of an evil witch.
Fear is you, in the middle of a fierce dream,
It looks like a big, fat, squishy tarantula, hanging from a
                                        haunted house wall.

**Emily-Jayne Court (8)**
**Sandford St Martin's CE VA First School**


# Excitement!

Excitement is as yellow and hot as the burning, beaming sun
                                        shining down on the earth.
It smells like ice cream which is cold and slippery.
Excitement is a person jumping on a hard, boingy trampoline,
It sounds like my cousin, shouting my name.
Excitement is going to a loud, noisy fairground,
It feels like a roller coaster or a *zooming* plane.
Excitement is Christmas, when all the cold, crispy snow is falling
                                        from the sky,
It tastes like a fizzy ice sundae melting in my mouth.

**Amy Hallett (8)**
**Sandford St Martin's CE VA First School**

## Happiness

Happiness is eating strawberries,
It smells like the fresh air by the seaside.
Happiness is tasty ice cream,
It sounds like lots of gorgeous blue balloons going off.
Happiness is my fun PS2,
It feels like a dog that feels like a beautiful, soft, silky sofa.
Happiness is my fluffy dog,
It tastes like the sweet scent of strawberries.
Happiness is chocolate ice cream,
It looks like glorious chocolate and the sun.

**Tom Henstridge (8)**
**Sandford St Martin's CE VA First School**


## Happiness

Happiness is sitting on a beach,
It smells like the salty sea.
Happiness is a wet swimming pool,
It sounds like someone jumping in a swimming pool.
Happiness is a shiny toy plane,
It feels like the side of a toy plane zooming along.
Happiness is a Mars bar,
It tastes like chocolate cake in my mouth.
Happiness is the sun,
It looks like it's burning in the sky.

**Sidney Burgess (7)**
**Sandford St Martin's CE VA First School**

## Happiness . . .

Happiness is the lovely sweet beautiful rose in my grandad's garden,
It smells like a lovely perfume in my nan's bedroom,
Happiness is Mrs Griffiths, playing on her piano,
It sounds like crashing music,
Happiness is like my teddy snuggling up to me,
If feels like a big piece of wool in a comfy ball,
Happiness is my nan's gorgeous roast dinner,
It tastes so appetising and good,
Happiness is the photo when I held Nan's hand at my mum's
Wedding before she died,
It looks like she enjoyed it,
I'm going to build a house.

**Danielle Wills (8)**
**Sandford St Martin's CE VA First School**


## Love

Love is like a graceful, sweet kiss in the air,
It smells like chocolates in a beautiful box,
Love is like a kind and delightful cuddle in the warm,
It sounds like pretty music in the air,
Love is like a charming dance, in the graceful moonlight,
It feels like a colourful dance, holding hands,
Love is a big cuddle,
It tastes like a strawberry-flavoured chocolate cake,
Love is a big cuddle for your family,
It looks like an excellent bird tweeting in the air.

**Ashleigh Jo Hall (8)**
**Sandford St Martin's CE VA First School**

## Happiness

Happiness is like friendly families coming,
It smells like Christmas cake for a little child to nibble at,
Happiness is like friendly clowns dancing and laughing,
It sounds like kind and careful friends chatting,
Happiness is like a smiling balloon waving to and fro,
It feels like a drop of golden sunshine,
Happiness is like happy thoughts coming,
It tastes like fresh yummy peaceful air,
Happiness is like the sound of people singing,
It looks like the sight of colours flashing around.

**Jade Fowler (8)**
**Sandford St Martin's CE VA First School**


## Happiness

Happiness is having lots of fun at baton twirling,
It smells like the boiling black sausages and like the night sky,
Happiness is getting warmed up at gymnastics,
It sounds like the balloon popping in my ear,
Happiness is friends that are kind to you,
It feels like my mum and my dad cuddling me,
Happiness is Mrs Griffiths letting us do easy work
And coming over to see our work,
It tastes like the yummy marshmallows sticking to
My teeth like chewing gum,
Happiness is clowns throwing pies at each other,
It looks like the sun and it shines like gold.

**Stephanie Lamb (8)**
**Sandford St Martin's CE VA First School**

## Shyness

Shyness is a bunch of flowers on my doorstep,
It smells like a sweet, summer breeze, on a cold day,
Shyness is somebody begging me to dance,
It sounds like a spray of music,
Shyness is a posy of new toys for my birthday,
It feels like a bunch of butterflies tickling my belly,
Shyness is like a little bit of water, going to my belly,
It tastes like a box of sweet chocolates,
Shyness is like going to do a show alone,
It looks like a huge crowd staring at me.

**Amy Webb (8)**
**Sandford St Martin's CE VA First School**


## Happiness

Happiness is to go on a very hot holiday,
It smells like a very delicious gammon cooking in the oven,
Happiness is like having your birthday,
It sounds like your favourite programme,
Happiness is like going to someone's party,
It feels like going on a scary roller coaster,
Happiness is like watching films in the cinema,
It tastes like a very sour sweet,
Happiness is like having a joyful dog,
It looks like watching a good swimmer.

**Henry Keep (7)**
**Sandford St Martin's CE VA First School**

## Happiness

Happiness is my favourite Bratz dolls,
It smells like my rose perfume,
Happiness is my yellow and white mountain bike,
It sounds like birds tweeting by my window,
Happiness is my auntie Maureen's wedding,
It feels like my stepmummy's cuddles,
Happiness is my new TV,
It tastes like my tasty pancakes,
Happiness is my sister when she laughs,
It looks like me when I'm dressing up.

**Casey Medley (7)**
**Sandford St Martin's CE VA First School**


## Fear

Fear is like a spider's web,
It smells like a raging burning fire,
Fear is like a T-rex ripping apart another dinosaur,
It sounds like a snake hissing in the jungle,
Fear is like a huge aeroplane crashing,
It feels like a bull thumping the ground behind me,
Fear is like a gunshot in the dark, night sky,
It tastes meaty on my plate,
Fear is like a high mountain,
It looks like a dinosaur wrecking the jungle.

**Ben Williams (7)**
**Sandford St Martin's CE VA First School**

## Happiness

Happiness is a big red balloon floating in the air,
It smells like fresh fish and chips that have just come out of the oven,
Happiness is travelling to my friend's house to play and have tea,
It sounds like someone is playing in my room,
Happiness is to go to school and play,
It feels like me playing with my friends,
Happiness is gobbling all kinds of sweets,
It tastes like me eating all of the chocolate,
Happiness is everyone playing together in class,
It looks like a huge big fair wheel going round.

**Will Joyce (7)**
**Sandford St Martin's CE VA First School**


## Shyness

Shyness is like talking in front of the school,
It smells like the salty sea fish,
Shyness is trying meat for the first time,
It sounds like people laughing at me,
Shyness is going to the beach for the first time,
It feels like touching the silky feathers of a bird,
Shyness is like playing football for the first time,
It tastes like lumpy chicken,
Shyness is drinking the sea,
It looks like people making fun of someone.

**Nathan Lee-Blues (8)**
**Sandford St Martin's CE VA First School**

# Happiness

Happiness is someone smiling back to me,
It smells like sweet, beautiful flowers,
Happiness is opening exciting presents from my birthday,
It sounds like a cat miaowing loudly in the hallway,
Happiness is when I play with my cute, cuddly cat,
It feels like playing with my special and only cat,
Happiness is when it's Easter time and we celebrate,
It tastes like delicious wonderful chocolate, yum-yum,
Happiness is when I can see my pleased best friends,
It looks like my likeable, kind and grateful friends,
Coming over to me.

**Stephanie Howard (7)**
**Sandford St Martin's CE VA First School**


# Happiness

Happiness is like someone at your doorstep,
With a box of chocolates,
It smells like a sweet rose that someone has given you,
Happiness is when you spend time with your family,
It sounds like someone saying something lovely about you,
Happiness is when you hang out with your friends,
It feels like you are warming a friend's heart by being considerate,
Happiness is yummy ice cream melting down your chubby chin,
It tastes like icy, flavoured, yummy, fluffy ice cream in my mouth,
Happiness is waking up on Christmas morning with a big yawn,
It looks like someone giving you something satisfying.

**Emily Kennedy (8)**
**Sandford St Martin's CE VA First School**

## Love

Love is like a tiny valentine's card,
It smells like some lovely hot chocolate fairy cakes,
Love is like a big bunch of flowers,
It sounds like a funny bird singing,
Love is like lovely pink and white marshmallows,
It feels like a loving dreamy dream,
Love is like a big pack of sweets,
It tastes like a huge box of strawberry chocolates,
Love is like a quiet lazy pet,
It looks like a soft gentle cuddle.

**Jade-Marie Shilling (7)**
**Sandford St Martin's CE VA First School**


## Love

Love is like a huge smile,
It smells like a hot dinner my mum gave to me,
Love is like my mum giving me a bright red rose,
It sounds like my mum saying 'I love you'.
I love is like my dad giving me a birthday card,
It feels like my mum giving me an enormous cuddle,
Love is like my mum taking me to the shops and
Holding my hand when I cross the road,
It tastes like a big roast dinner my dad's cooked me,
Love is like my dad reading me a bedtime story,
It looks like my mum giving me a toy.

**Jamie Harkins (7)**
**Sandford St Martin's CE VA First School**

## Shyness

Shyness is like going somewhere familiar,
Your curiosity getting the better of you.
It smells like the cleaning products,
Curious where they are kept.
Shyness is like the poor mice,
Who can't survive the mousetraps.
It sounds like my friends whispering mean things about me
When we fall out.
Shyness is like a sky-blue teardrop falling from my eye, when I blush.
It feels like lots of coldness, as I cuddle my new teddy.
Shyness is like scared birds,
Whose sharp ears could hear a stick crack.
It tastes like the sour, new taste of juice,
Whilst it's running down your chin.
Shyness is the way you are, when you've got a new teacher,
Especially when they're bossy.
It looks like the other shy children blushing,
When strangers stare and make their feet sink in the ground,
Glued with five layers of cement.

**Rhiannon Davies (8)**
**Sandford St Martin's CE VA First School**


## Happiness

Happiness is like a hard balloon,
It smells like a good cup of orange,
Happiness is winning a football match,
It sounds like a bird whistling,
Happiness is sharing with people,
It feels like a nice feather,
Happiness is helping people with their work,
It tastes like a juicy apple,
Happiness is giving people money,
It looks like a huge piece of candyfloss.

**Daniel Bray (8)**
**Sandford St Martin's CE VA First School**

## Untold Future

What will unfold in our future?
Will there be another horrifying World War again,
Or maybe there will be world peace once more.
Perhaps there will be funky new inventions,
We could go to space for school trips,
We could even have aliens for tourist guides!
New plans might be made for stopping awful pollution,
Inventors can create excellent new inventions,
With new species
That can be found in the most unusual places,
Previously unknown islands can be found,
With new food and lovely juicy fruits,
Great new plants and flowers might grow,
Will you be happy
When you know what's in store for us humans?
What will happen in our destiny?

**Alanna Sibbald (10)**
**The Priory CE VA Primary School**


## Earth's Future

Is the future black and bad?
I see that and feel very sad,
So we need to find a better place,
Does it come from outer space?
No . . . here on Earth we have to stay,
And hope we don't get washed away,
The Arctic is melting due to pollution,
'Clean up our act,' that's the solution,
Will all animals fly and have no feet?
Unlike the dodo who got beat!
We need to take care and not neglect,
Show our planet better respect,
We want our world a happier place to be,
For everyone including me!

**Abbie Denison (9)**
**The Priory CE VA Primary School**

## A Poem About The World's Future!

I wanted the world to be a happy place,
Not filled with lots of pollution,
Maybe some new animals,
Not hunting that leads to extinction.

Not a disastrous thing,
Like a third world war,
I disagree with terrorist attacks,
Please, we want *no* more.

I hope our weather settles down
And global warming stops,
Then acid rain is no more,
To bring back sweet raindrops.

As we spin round and round,
In our orbit out in space,
I hope that in a thousand years,
This is still a wonderful place.

**Jack Brickell (9)**
The Priory CE VA Primary School

## The Year 2026

The year 2026
What will it hold?
Global warming,
New technology.

The year 2026
What will it be?
Hover cars or robots
Round every corner.

Will it be space trips to Mars
And see the moon?
Will every house
Have a widescreen TV?

**George Burgess (9)**
The Priory CE VA Primary School

# What If?

What if the bombs came again,
Would we have time to build a shelter?
What if 9/11 happened again,
Would we have time to pray?
What we need is world peace and hope for every day.

What if carbon monoxide increases,
Will butterflies continue to flutter?
What if the powerful tiger is hunted,
Will it be a memory for only a few?
What we need is co-operation from around the world.

What if explorers went to unknown places,
Would we find animals and insects new?
What if a new flower was found,
Would cancer be cured?
What we need is clever people's help from around the world.

What if new technology expands,
Will it save a new baby's life?
What if new technology makes the ozone layer thinner,
Will the UV rays destroy us?
What we need is world's agreement.

What if we saved a lot of energy,
Will it stop a lot of pollution?
What if we used the bins more,
Will it prevent litter?
What we need is people's promise to keep the world clean.

What if we stopped hunting,
Will it help the animals to live longer?
What if we just believed in each other's religions,
Will it bring an end to most world wars?
What we need is everyone's love and care.

*What if we saved the world?*

**Abigail Watts (9)**
**The Priory CE VA Primary School**

# Earth's Future!

If I went to the year 4000,
Will there be new technology, with cars flying round in the air?
As people carry on working, and then stop and stare?
Or is there going to be peace spread around the world,
How do we know?
How do we find out?
We can't we don't know.

Will there be global warming without any warning?
So if taps are dripping, lights are switching . . . on,
What's the solution to global pollution?

Is there nothing we can do?
So what do we do?
Where do we start?
Well, you don't need to be a genius,
For a start, turn off a light, you're saving electricity,
If a whole school did that, do you realise how
Much less pollution there will be?
Absolutely loads!

If you have a bin then use it,
Don't throw litter on the floor,
It doesn't take much!

So why don't we all help?
It's easy, even turning off a light can help!
So help now!

**Olivia Bisson-Simmonds (10)**
**The Priory CE VA Primary School**

## The Recipe For A Perfect World

Shoppers flee from atomic car bombs,
Passing streets and alleyways drowned in pollution,
Whilst rainforest animals are on the brink of extinction,
Is this how our world should be?
The old man remembers the world when he was young,
The world that made Earth what it is now,
But now there are more wars,
Theme parks and broken ozone,
The icebergs are melting,
The Antarctic is in danger,
And it's all because of you and me,
That's right! You reading this now,
And me - writing to you.
We are the ones who can take care of the future,
We can save energy and ensure world peace,
We can turn lights off when they're on for no reason,
But to do so we must be nice,
Be nice to the animals that we are affecting,
Be nice to the prisoners and victims of war,
Let's help all the people!
And let's save our future!
Make the world we have now into much, much more,
Get new technology,
Find new animals,
Stop all pollution and chances of war!
And the finished product is a beautiful world.

**Sophie Pope (10)**
**The Priory CE VA Primary School**

## The Year 4073

I wonder how different the world will be
In the year four thousand and seventy three?

Lasers could come and zap us away,
To the strangest of plants for the whole of the day.

We could fly to the moon for the day and back -
It can't get much more exciting than that!

Will there be robots acting as slaves,
And will there be such things as space aeroplanes?

Will the cow and the horse become extinct?
Now that is something to make you think!

Global warming could reach a stage,
Where we either fry or have an ice age!

There's no more work and no more school,
Life's become a lot less cruel!

Factory people fling open the gates -
From boring jobs they can now escape.

There's no disease and no more war,
People are living many years more.

At the end of the day, we can never quite tell,
What lies ahead and perhaps it's just as well!

**Lauren Beech (9)**
**The Priory CE VA Primary School**


## My Pet Husky

My pet husky is the colour of the moon,
He's sweet and sour and as loud as a drum,
His big nose is like a leather coat,
And his big eyes are like diamonds.
He's a hunter howling, like a singing bird in the sky.

**Isobel Booth (8)**
**The Priory CE VA Primary School**

## What Will Be Our World's Future?

Will our world be a nice place,
Or will it be dull and sad?

Will it be healthy and peaceful,
Or polluted, ruined and bad?

Will the sun be as bright,
Or will the Earth be so dark?

Will all the children die of disease,
Or take long school trips to Mars?

Will my family be merely dead,
Or will we all be alive?

Will there be flying motor cars,
Or will we still have to drive?

Will the animals be extinct,
Or will they just hide away?

Will there be fun new inventions,
Or just the same as today?

I do not know what will happen,
But I do know one thing for sure,

That if we are not very careful,
There will be no world to explore!

**Joanna Wassell (10)**
The Priory CE VA Primary School

## Husky

Stormy black nose,
Blanket-fluffy tail
Inky-blue eyes
Cloudy grey-black coat
Paper-white tummy
Flower-pink tongue.

**Elizabeth Lovett (8)**
The Priory CE VA Primary School

## What Will Happen To Our World In The Future?

Our world could be more exciting,
With friendly robots and flying cars,
And planes that can go into space,
Or trains that don't need a driver.

Our world could be more peaceful,
No wars, no murders and no attacks,
Destroying all lethal weapons,
So it's safe to walk out at night.

Our world could get warmer,
From pollution from cars and buses,
And smoke from factory chimneys,
Even TV and light pollution.

Our world could have new species,
Colourful fish and birds,
And new breeds of cat and dog,
Even the Loch Ness Monster!

Our world could be cleaner,
Without rubbish and junk,
And no chewing gum on our streets,
What a brilliant world it *could* be!

**Jim Gerrard (10)**
**The Priory CE VA Primary School**


## Extinction

Slaughtering our animals is so cruel,
Why do we do such things?
We blitz one species and they become endangered,
If we continue to bombard our endangered species
They will become extinct!

Stop hunting and destroying their homes,
We can survive without.

**Jake Fell (10)**
**The Priory CE VA Primary School**

## What We Do

I hope you know what we humans are doing,
We're polluting the world,
We are being litterbugs by dropping litter,
We are killing animals and going on safaris.

*Stop coming on safaris,
You're ruining our home.
My sister and I are petrified of those flashing lights.
Please stop coming, that's all we ask.*

What we do is horrible,
I can hardly breathe.
We pollute by using cars.
Please walk somewhere,
It's healthy.

Stop, halt, pick up your litter,
You're hurting the poor animals,
You're cutting down more trees,
You could recycle cans or paper.

That's how you can help,
So you better do it.
So now you know,
What us humans do.

**Rebecca Simpson (10)**
**The Priory CE VA Primary School**


## The Future

New fashions, groovy hair,
Flying cars and hoverchairs,
All TVs will be 3D,
Great fun for you and me,
Robots used to clean and cook,
So we can sit and read a book,
The future's great for you and me,
Happiness eternally.

**Elliot Wilks (9)**
**The Priory CE VA Primary School**

## The Future Of The World

What will the Earth be like in the future?
Will there be species I have never seen?
Will there be tourism?
I would like to know, what is held in the future?

Will there be wars,
With bombs crashing down?
Is the future ideal or sad?
I will never know.

What will the teachers teach to the children?
Will there be school,
Or are we born clever?
This I don't know.

I know what I want,
You know what you want,
We don't know what God wants,
That's the mystery.

The future,
A scary thought!
What will the future be like?

**Emily Fardell (10)**
**The Priory CE VA Primary School**


## The World's Future

What might happen in the future?
More terrorist attacks,
There might be another world war,
Even more pollution,
And the ozone's breaking up!

What might happen in the future?
World peace would be nice,
We might find new species,
Some new technology could be discovered,
Or endangered animals could be extinct!

**Emily Gola (9)**
**The Priory CE VA Primary School**

## The Future Through My Eyes

Who knows what the future could hold,
Holidays in space and cures for the cold,
New technology like hovering cars,
With magnificent creatures,
With necks like giraffes,
Terrorist attacks,
They really worry me,
Could this be the start,
Or World War three?
Global warming is an awful matter,
It gets quite freaky,
To know the ozone may shatter,
It smells quite fumy when cars go past,
They use too much petrol,
And go away too fast,
We need to think today,
For the children of tomorrow,
The future is a way,
So we need to limit sorrow.

**Sam Pitman (10)**
**The Priory CE VA Primary School**


## The Future

Come, come the future's begun,
Like a marching band and a deafening drum,
Like a deep, gloomy mist it sweeps the land,
Changing past into present and making good from bad.

In years to come the world will change,
We should not be scared but strong and brave,
Like the memories of our family passed,
The future has come at last, at last.

I have no idea of what the future will hold,
So we will wait for the hands of time to unfold.
Whether there will be many robots or flying cars,
What is now just thoughts shall soon be ours.

**Louis Rice (10)**
**The Priory CE VA Primary School**

## The World

Our world is not yet wrecked and ruined,
But we can make a difference by stopping all the litter,
Thrown on the floor
And not use too much hairspray, it's not happened yet but
The ozone will fall apart,
And if that happens then we will all freeze,
It's sad to hear about hunting because sooner or later
The animals that have been hunted will be extinct,
But we can do something about it and even something small
Can make a big change and make the bad go away.

The war has started to appear and that is not a good sign
And world peace is not going to happen if we carry on
Voting yet to the war,
So say no and stop the war,
If the war does happen, it's another thing that's damaged
Our precious world,
Like hunting and littering is making our world fall apart,
Our world needs to be helped a lot,
To make it a better place and not be a horrible one,
If our world is to kept clean, then we will die and more
Scientists will find more disease,
But with a little help and time,
The scientists will find more cures for diseases,
It will be a better world and place,
And a much happier, safer and cleaner place at that!

**Nicola Brown (10)**
The Priory CE VA Primary School


## Polar Bear

Damp, sweet, slippery, sliding, snow where a polar bear may live.
Feet like fast, fluffy clouds.
Sharp, spiky spikes stuck on the feet like a brush.
There's a wet nose like a puddle in a field.
Big bear bouncing around.
A belly like a pillow.

**Lucy Cherrett (8)**
The Priory CE VA Primary School

## My Hopes And Wishes For The World

My hopes and wishes for the world,
Are that poverty will disappear.
My hopes and wishes for the world,
Are that children will not live in fear.

The world would be a better place,
If guns and weapons were swept away.
The world would be a better place,
If refugees could have their say.

We could improve the world,
By spreading the food around.
We could improve the world,
By growing crops up from the ground.

I can help the world,
By using less electricity.
I can help the world,
By saving power and energy.

**Lydia Bassett (9)**
**The Priory CE VA Primary School**


## The Future

The future might be nice or,
It might be bad,
There might be a war,
That would be sad.
It could be fun,
But we need to do a little job,
Then you can lounge in the sun,
Do not be a slob,
'Turn off the electricity Son,'
Will say Dad,
'Then have your fun.'

**Aaron Rackstraw (10)**
**The Priory CE VA Primary School**

# If We Tried, We Could Change The World

I see a terrible world but that could change if we *tried*
F ur being found in a bag. That could change if we *tried.*

W ar carries on. That could change if we *tried*
E xtinction for the animals. That could change if we *tried.*

T errorist attacks could stop. Only if *they* tried
R eal guns banned from teenagers could stop. *We all* could try
I f we stopped pollution, that would save animals *lives*
E very person throwing their rubbish in the *bin*, that would help
D eodorants and sprays *banned*, that would help people's *lives.*

W orld peace. That would change the *world*
E veryone recycling. That would help the *animals.*

C oke cans could turn into another can if we *recycled*
O zone layer could break down if we don't ban *sprays*
U nder the ocean. Remember that it's *there*
L itterbins could increase if we *tried*
D ogs and other pets treated *properly.*

C heetahs and other animals set *free*
H itting children hard *banned*
A nimals treated like *animals*
N ew technology made. That could change the *world*
G lobal warming could stop if we *tried*
E lectricity saved. That would help *everyone.*

T errorists attacks stopped. That would bring peace to the *world*
H oses and taps turned off *properly*
E xtra food left over on your plate, don't put it in the *rubbish.*

W indows and doors shut. That would help save *electricity*
O ld things could be new things if we *recycle* more
R hinos being hunted for their skin again can make them extinct
L ots of fish were taken away from their *real* home to be sold
D ifferent ideas to change the world and make it into a good place
 . . . it could come true if we all *tried.*

**Cloe Brunerie (10)**
**The Priory CE VA Primary School**

## Is World War III The Only Future?

The first bomb hit,
The whole world shook,
Slicing through the air they came,
Demolishing anything that dared stand in their way.
A screaming shell,
Slammed to the ground,
Blood and limbs scattered all over the floor.

A surprising horror was now reality,
Was I the only one?
Desolate and ravaged landscape all around.
I cowered low into the ground,
Not letting anyone see me,
If there were any left,
Dreading what would happen next.
Is this the reality of the future?

**Hannah Arkell (10)**
**The Priory CE VA Primary School**


## The Future

What is the future going to be like?
What is in store?
Maybe new inventions,
I will have to wait and see,
Maybe a new robot?
Maybe a talking tree?
They could find new animals,
We will have to wait and see,
There might be jumping snakes,
There could be mechanical rakes,
There might be flying pigs,
Maybe 100 metre long wigs,
Lots and lots of things,
It is up to us to help the future,
And now let's just wait and see.

**Joseph Alexander (10)**
**The Priory CE VA Primary School**

## What Will The Future Be Like For Me?

What will the future be like for me?
Will there still be any trees?

Will there be another war?
Will some countries still be poor?

Will the inventors be really busy,
Making rocket cars that will make us feel dizzy?

Will we have school trips to Mars?
Will we find some lost stars?

I wish I had a machine that could travel through time,
To answer all these questions of mine.

Maybe I could find the solution
To stop all of this terrible pollution.

I could stop global warming
By giving everyone a warning.

Maybe I could suddenly find
A brand-new animal that is loving and kind.

If only I could help the world more
By making the rich people give to the poor.

If only I could stop things getting so bad
Because the future to me looks quite sad!

**Jordan Puttick (9)**
**The Priory CE VA Primary School**


## Polar Bear In The Sunset

A big, fluffy female bear, prowling around silently,
The cold fiery sunset hiding behind the sky,
A nice cosy coat to keep her warm all through the night and day.
She strikes into the sea.
Icy icicles around the ocean like a cold dark room.
Tearing away at her prey like a fierce animal.
On land now, she's running back to feed her family.
Night comes and they all fall asleep, not making a sound . . .

**Melissa Stocker (8)**
**The Priory CE VA Primary School**

## What Does The Future Hold

We will have to wait,
And see what goes on,
Through the centuries,
To see what the future holds.

Perhaps there will be,
An end to violence
People will care for others,
Peace on Earth will come.

Just think before you drop litter,
Before you get in your car,
Can you recycle any more?
Think what you're doing to the world.

Poor creatures being tormented,
The planet's being polluted,
It's our entire fault,
The time to stop is *now*.

Stop having enemies,
Just respect one another,
We are all neighbours
All over the world.

So if we do this,
No more horrifying wars will go on,
There will be peace,
And an end to spitefulness.

**India Dale (10)**
**The Priory CE VA Primary School**


## Arctic Scene

Shining silver seals with eyes like goggles,
Speeding like a speedboat,
Flippy flexible fish,
Bright, cold dolphins,
Cunning little polar bears.

**Edward Burt (8)**
**The Priory CE VA Primary School**

# The Year 3000

Y ou can grow huge yellow bananas as long as arms
E verywhere there will be theme parks
A ll adults act like children
R ain never falls in the summer

T abby cats never run away
H ouses that self clean
R ats that are not harmful
E veryone has their own robot
E verywhere there will be happy people

T here are cars that hover
H orses that can fly
O ysters that always carry pearls
U FOs landing on the planet Earth
S isters that are clever and kind
A nts the size of centipedes
N o one ever goes in their cellar
D ads come home early to play.

**Callum Heath (10)**
**The Priory CE VA Primary School**


# Underneath The Big Blue Sea

Underneath the big blue sea
I can see,
Sleepy, snowy-white seals,
Clever, careful, cold cubs,
Round blue eyes like my bouncy ball,
Flexible, friendly fast seals swimming in the calm sea,
Tall, noisy seals,
Happy, funny seals.
That is what I can see in the big blue sea.

**Rachel Hawkins (8)**
**The Priory CE VA Primary School**

## The Future

The future is clear now,
The sun rises with world peace by its side,
No more dying or killing
No more wars causing countries to divide,

No more Third World poverty,
No unhappiness, hunger or hurt,
No more natural disasters,
Grass grows now, where once there was dirt,

Shelter for all,
New life is found,
No more terror to endure,
Theme parks spring up from the ground,

Diseases have ended,
Cancer is no more,
No need for medicine or hospitals
As we have found the cure,

At school there are no bullies,
Education is still great,
Computers are what we use every day,
And that's something to celebrate.

In my town there are no more small shops,
Separate shops to buy sweets, bread and meat,
However now there is only one big shop,
With everything you need to eat.

In this future there is everything you have dreamed,
Feelings of fun, happiness and love,
We could make this happen,
It's up to us and a little help from God above.

**Mason Doick (10)**
**The Priory CE VA Primary School**